the ANTIQUE
MYSTIQUE
GUIDE TO SOUTHERN ONTARIO

Three-drawer side table in tiger maple.

the ANTIQUE MYSTIQUE

GUIDE TO SOUTHERN ONTARIO

Kathy McCleary
Photography by Gord Handley

Stoddart

A BOSTON MILLS PRESS BOOK

Canadian Cataloguing in Publication Data

McCleary, Kathy, 1951-
    The antique mystique guide to southern Ontario

ISBN 1-55046-089-7

1. Antique dealers - Ontario - Directories. I. Title.

NK1127.M33 1994   381'.457451'025713   C94-930262-7

First published in 1994 by
Stoddart Publishing Co. Limited
34 Lesmill Road
Toronto, Canada
M3B 2T6
(416) 445-3333

A BOSTON MILLS PRESS BOOK
The Boston Mills Press
132 Main Street
Erin, Ontario
N0B 1T0

Design by Mary Firth
Printed in Hong Kong

The publisher gratefully acknowledges the support of The Canada Council, Ontario Ministry of Culture and Communications, Ontario Arts Council, and Ontario Publishing Centre in the development of writing and publishing in Canada.

BACK COVER PHOTOS (CLOCKWISE FROM TOP LEFT): Goblet from Country Lane Antiques. New England Sheraton-style field bed in birch and maple with original cherry stain, circa 1840, from High House Antiques. A Louis XIII-style table, circa 1720, from Hinton Antiques. A wooden butter bowl full of treenware, including butter ladles, butter prints and mashers, from Pine and Time Antiques.

Mary Gregory-style glass, such as this from Black Shutter Antiques, was made by many different companies.

Acknowledgments

Sincerest thanks to all the antique dealers for sharing their thoughts so openly and generously and for the cups of tea and sweets that kept two travellers fuelled.

Thanks to fellow traveller and life companion, Richard, whose contribution to this book cannot be measured.

Thanks to publisher John Denison for bringing this idea to me in the first place.

Thanks to photographer Gord Handley, who proves that old adage about pictures and words.

"Antique Mystique" is the title of my column which has appeared weekly in *The Woodbridge Advertiser* since 1987. Thanks to that newspaper's publishers, Beverley and Karl Mallette, for their enthusiasm over this project.

Thanks to editor Sarah Reid for her helpful advice.

Greenburnie Antiques can help you create an elegant setting.

Contents

Introduction

Have you ever wanted to spend a leisurely afternoon antique-hunting but didn't know where to go? Have you ever wanted a specific piece of Canadiana and didn't know where to find it? Have you ever wondered how to recognize a reputable antique dealer? Wonder no more: this guidebook has the answers. Fifty Ontario dealers could not be assembled who collectively know more about Canadian antiques.

The dealers in the following pages were chosen for inclusion by a consensus of their peers. They specialize in every piece of antiquity Canada has to offer, from crocks and lamps and decoys, to vintage clothing and books, to country and formal furniture. They span Southern Ontario—city, country, and small town. These men and women have accumulated expertise that comes only with years of experience and study. In these pages they pass some of their knowledge on to you. Reading this book and visiting these dealers should make the whole mysterious search for that special treasure easier and more rewarding.

There is a mystique surrounding every antique. Where has it been? Who fashioned it? What were the circumstances of the creator's life? For whom was it made and when? Who else has owned it?

You purchase the item, incorporate it into your home, and part of your enjoyment, something you can only vaguely comprehend, floats in the air around it. The very age of an antique lends it a certain aura.

The fifty dealers interviewed for this book have each made a concentrated effort to explore those mysteries of antiquity whenever and wherever they can. Ethically and enthusiastically they have pursued the puzzles of Canadiana, unravelling solutions. They understand that you have to touch and feel and smell antiques in order to know them. They appreciate that you must do this over a long period of time. Every time you purchase something and then live with it, your nose gets that much better for sniffing out the good stuff. It's a bit like "having a good eye" in baseball. A player with a good eye knows when he's staring at a strike pitch and knows that he'd better swing or else he's out. Baseball players are not born with good eyes; they develop them through playing ball with the best coaches.

I hope this introduction to fifty of Ontario's foremost antique coaches will help you play ball in the antiques game. When you're travelling any distance to visit them, a call ahead is always recommended.

SOUTHERN GEORGIAN BAY

A tilt-top Maritime candle stand in tiger maple among other garden treasures at McCleary's Antiques in Avening.

1

McCleary's Antiques
Embarking on an Adventure

Searching for Canadian country furniture has been an adventure for my husband Richard and me. I grew up in a family of antique collectors, and Richard and I met in 1967. When his job took us to Montreal we began to furnish our home in antiques. We found that we liked French Canada—its antiques and its people.

But the pastime got out of hand, as the antiques hobby will, and in 1975, when we returned to Ontario, we opened McCleary's Antiques in Cookstown. Ten years later we purchased the general store in Avening and moved our enterprise to larger quarters. Our specialty has always been pre-Confederation furniture from Ontario and Quebec, and we search for real quality in our Canadian country furnishings.

Eighteenth-century Quebec armoire with carved diamond point panels.

There are four important things to consider when viewing any piece: age, originality, craftsmanship (in both construction and embellishments), and provenance.

Age is simple—the older a piece is, the better.

Originality involves two things. The piece should have little or no repair, and it should retain its original finish. What if you don't like original finishes? It's a personal thing. Our preference is for painted pieces, but our adventure may be different than yours. If you like refinished furniture, buy refinished furniture. If it was crafted with quality and refinished properly, there will always be a market for that piece.

How do you recognize quality in craftsmanship? It goes right back to the ability of the cabinetmaker. Examine any case piece, be it a dish dresser, a corner cupboard or a wardrobe (*armoire* and *shranke* are the French and German terms). With English and German pieces, look for dovetailed construction in drawers and casements (the body of the cupboard). With French furniture, you should expect to find the casement built with a corner-post construction: four square wooden posts to which the cupboard frame is joined with a rabbetted (grooved) or mortise-and-tenon (notched) joint, secured with wooden pegs.

What other details could you look for in a well-crafted cupboard? Glazed cupboards (that is, cupboards with glass doors) should feature raised mullions—the divisions between the panes. With blind cupboards (cupboards with solid doors), you should find moulded panelling. Look for details such as beading around doors and drawers (a small half-moon detail usually made by planing a groove in the frame, but sometimes applied), or lapped doors and

A Mennonite corner cupboard dated 1843 vies for attention with a striking Star of Bethlehem quilt, circa late 1800s.

drawers (doors and drawers which aren't flush with the frame, but overlap it). Picture-frame mouldings (applied mouldings that go around the outer edge of the face of the piece) provide interest, as do fielded panels (panels bevelled around the outside edge to fit into a groove in the door frame). Early cabinetmakers liked to embellish their cupboards with an interesting foot and cornice. These are a few examples of details that show a good craftsman was at work.

The fourth consideration is provenance, the history of the piece. Who made it? When? Where? What family did it belong to?

If you look for age, originality, craftsmanship, and provenance, and you find them all, then you have discovered a great piece of Canadian country furniture. What if you don't find all four? Which of the four is the most important? There is no order of importance. You must weigh each quality separately to come up with a total assessment of worth.

When you embark on the quest for quality country furniture, nothing remains static. You might move to a different region of the country. Your taste might change. Nonetheless, if you buy with the above criteria in mind, then you can always upgrade or change your furniture without losing your investment.

You often can't control events in your life, but you can always make your collecting hobby an adventure.

McCleary's Antiques:
Richard and Kathy McCleary
Avening, one hour north of Toronto on Airport Road
Open weekends 10:00 A.M. – 5:00 P.M., weekdays please call ahead
(705) 466-3019

As you travel, visiting antique shops, you should also take in our many and varied museums. Ask the dealers to tell you where local museums are located. There is something to be learned at every one of them.

2

Belhaven Antiques
Signed Tiffany Glass

"Browsers Welcome" reads the sign in front of Belhaven Antiques in Creemore, and it has been a standing invitation to customers for eight years now. Follow the path and you'll find a charmed world of flowing water and quiet forest—and some of the finest pieces of glass ever made.

Though you will discover formal furnishings and jewellery at this shop, along with some country furniture, Lindsay Bell and partner Wayne Winters have a special interest in lamps. Not just any lamps, but lamps from the first twenty years of this century. Simpler designs were a reaction to the overdone Victorian era when clutter reigned. Craftsmen such as Tiffany, Steuben, Quezall, Handel, Fosteria and Pairpoint were the primary North American glass designers of this period.

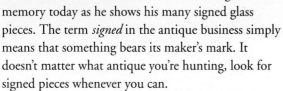

Lindsay still remembers the first time he was offered "signed" pieces of Tiffany glass. "Why didn't they have a hand-written signature if they were signed?" he wanted to know. Still, the lamp shades were indeed quite lovely, and they were stamped *Tiffany,* so he bought them. He laughs at that memory today as he shows his many signed glass pieces. The term *signed* in the antique business simply means that something bears its maker's mark. It doesn't matter what antique you're hunting, look for signed pieces whenever you can.

A few tips from Lindsay about Tiffany lamps:

Tiffany has become a generic term for a much-copied style of glass. Real Tiffany was made by Louis Comfort Tiffany in his glass works in Corona, New York. Back then, Tiffany was the highest quality lighting you could buy, and although it was made in large quantities it was always a commodity for the well-to-do. In fact, Tiffany was considered the best American glassmaker of his time. Only signed Tiffany pieces are valuable. He used the marks *L.C.T., L.C. Tiffany,* and *Louis C. Tiffany,* and sometimes the word *Favrille.* His bronze lamp bases are of the finest form and are also signed *Tiffany.*

Tiffany, son of the famous New York jeweller, used designs based on nature to create luxury in lighting. Lindsay has fashioned a setting for his shop that is natural yet elegant, much like the style of glass that he values most.

Belhaven Antiques:
Lindsay Bell and Wayne Winters
West of Creemore on County Road 9
Open 10:00 A.M. – 5:00 P.M. every day except Christmas
(705) 466-3368

Favourite references:
The Glass of Frederick Carder, Paul V. Gardner
American Art Nouveau Glass, Albert Christian Revi

Also in Creemore:
Old Sport Company
Antique Sporting Memorabilia

14

ABOVE: *The most brilliant light that money could buy in 1910; bases all signed* Tiffany Studios, New York; *glass shades all signed* L.C. Tiffany, Favrille.
FACING PAGE: *A signed Four Seasons Pairpoint base and shade illuminate a summer country scene.*

3

Country House Antiques

What Is an Antique Dealer?

What is an antique dealer? A modern gypsy travelling about the countryside? A material archivist and librarian for the future? A collector whose passion for purchasing antiques got out of control?

Martha Todd and Joyce Wright aren't quite sure. They do know that they love doing what they do. In fact, they can't imagine anything as diverse, interesting or as stimulating as dealing in antiques.

You can share their enthusiasm at their Country House, a rebuilt log structure on the beautiful west shore of Lake Simcoe. They run their business by appointment only, because they want to take their time with each customer. This is how they have worked for fifteen years. Their wares, pre-Confederation Canadian painted country furniture and ethnic furniture, plus woodenware and other accessories, are in original or restored-to-original condition.

Don't forget that Canadian country folk painted their furniture initially. They painted it in an attempt to upgrade the pine, a wood they considered to be inferior. Sometimes they painted it with a mock woodgrain simulating more expensive indigenous woods such as bird's-eye and tiger maple. Sometimes they copied the colours and grains of more exotic woods from warmer climes, such as West Indies mahogany. Sometimes they painted it a colour— shades of red, blue, green, yellow. Sometimes they chose combinations of these.

When the personality of the maker is revealed, Martha and Joyce consider the piece folk art. Why try to define the term any further, they ask. A folk artist looks at a block of wood and sees something in it. Perhaps it's a figure. Perhaps it's a wall shelf or a water bird or a butter print. Perhaps it's a cupboard. The artist creates what he sees, and the paint is part of that.

Should you buy an antique because you think it will appreciate in value? Martha and Joyce think not. Buy it because it has a certain quietude about it, an aura, if you will, a harmony and a voice or character of its own. Buy it because it will be useful to you. Buy it because you like it. If it appreciates—and it probably will—then that's a bonus, isn't it?

Country House Antiques:
Martha Todd and Joyce Wright
Near Hawkestone on Lakeshore Road between
Oro Line 13 and the Orillia–Oro Town Line on
Lake Simcoe
By appointment
(705) 325-0183

ABOVE: Early Canadian country pieces in the perfect log cabin setting.

RIGHT: Common barnyard animals are elevated to an art form by their folk creators.

FACING PAGE: Downstairs at County House Antiques, where folk art is a favourite.

4

Hinton Antiques
Tangible History

If you want to be able to touch history, visit an antique store. So says Stephen Hinton, a history teacher and an antique dealer for twenty-two years. Examples of your country's earliest furniture may reveal solutions to mysteries of your heritage. Touch these pieces—pieces fashioned of wood from the bountiful forests that first covered this land and you'll touch their makers, the pioneers.

French King Louis IV was among the first to see Canada as a place of settlement. In 1663 Louis proclaimed Quebec a royal province of France. Blue and gold were the French royal colours. Is it any wonder that so many French armoires were painted blue? And those carvings that look like shells on early French cupboards? They were sunbursts carved in remembrance of the sun king, across the sea in France.

Following British conquest in 1759, New France ceased to exist as a political entity, but it wasn't until after the American Revolution that the English, in the form of United Empire Loyalists, began to place their English–American stamp on the land. Look at their furniture and it will tell the story of that wave of settlers. They were prosperous. They knew who they were and what they believed in. They were well rewarded for their loyalty to Britain.

Stephen's own hometown is Atherley, where Hintons have lived since 1870. To the east lies Mara Township. In 1847, two years after the great potato

RIGHT: A bow-front corner cupboard (late 18th century) from Quebec.
FACING PAGE: Obvious Pennsylvania German influence exudes from this early 19th-century dish cupboard at left.

famine struck Ireland, a hundred thousand Irish settlers arrived in Canada. Many of them settled in Mara Township. If we study their furniture, we can better understand the struggle they faced. They built practical, multipurpose pieces such as dish dressers that stood by the hearth and held everything the family owned: dishes, pots, pails—and under the high-cut bottom doors there was even room for a nesting hen! Irish tables had double stretchers underneath so that things could be stored across them. Before a burial, the coffin would be placed here. Settle beds served as benches by day and beds at night. Such furniture illustrates that practicality ruled.

To the west of Stephen and wife Wendy's home once ran the "Ridge Road" joining Barrie to Orillia. Along it English soldiers who had distinguished themselves in the War of 1812 were given land grants. To the north of Atherley, the Scottish settled.

Antique buffs who collect this country's historical artifacts should remember that settlement in each area of Canada was distinctive. There are rare and beautiful things to be found in every region.

Stephen and Wendy Hinton are adamant: in Canada, we have a unique country furniture tradition. We don't have to take a back seat to anyone.

Hinton Antiques:
Stephen and Wendy Hinton
65 Queen Street, Atherley
By appointment
(705) 325-9666

Favourite references:
Loyal She Remains, United Empire Loyalist Society
All About Ontario Tables, also *All About Ontario Chairs*, *All About Ontario Beds*, *All About Ontario Chests*, and *All About Ontario Desks*, a series of booklets about Ontario furniture, by Elizabeth Ingolfsrud.

5

The Swan Shop and John Poole Antiques
Reclaiming Antiques

Finding and reclaiming something of value in things that are lost are among the rewards of antique-hunting. In 1977, John and Mary Poole discovered a former antique store for sale in Craighurst. They knew they could give The Swan Shop the tender loving care needed to restore it. The building had the distinction of being the oldest standing structure in Flos Township. The owner, Phil Newman, had only one request. He wanted the name, The Swan Shop, to continue. Now run exclusively by Mary, The Swan Shop does continue.

Mary's art background makes her approach to antiques unique. She looks on early Canadian pieces as "functional sculptures." These are creations, she says. Antiques don't have to fill your house or even a room in your house. They can stand on their own, like works of art.

RIGHT: At home in The Swan Shop garden.
FACING PAGE: John Poole's carefully reclaimed antiques.

The Swan Shop specializes in country furniture and accessories, incorporated with arts and crafts by local artists. Finding something that has been abused or discarded by its former owner, reclaiming it, and making it a thing of beauty again is Mary's ongoing passion.

A short drive north on historic Highway 93 brings you to Hillsdale, where you'll find John, the former co-owner of The Swan Shop, now operating John Poole Antiques.

John grew up in upstate New York, and his parents collected country furniture. It seemed natural to continue searching out antiques when he moved to Canada, and he has been a full-time antique dealer since 1975. John Poole Antiques specializes in pre-Confederation country furniture from the Ottawa Valley and Quebec, refinished, in original finishes, or "as found."

Along with the antique business, John operates a custom refinishing shop. His many years of experience enable him to give this simple advice about refinishing antiques: don't overdo anything. Be gentle when using your scraper and your sander. Leaving the paint stripper on too long can cause damage to the wood. Strip the piece layer by layer, and if you can preserve the colour which the piece was originally painted, by all means do so. Dry scraping is one method of saving original colours. If you can't save the first colour, at least take care to preserve the wood's natural patina.

Wood takes on a distinctive hue over the years. White pine, for example, attains a golden glow. Saving this patina is very important when refinishing, and oversanding will remove this naturally aged layer of wood. Choose your finish carefully, and take the time to prepare for each coat properly. Remember, restoration is a skill that requires care and patience.

Exterior of John Poole Antiques

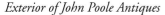

The Swan Shop:
Mary Poole, Craighurst
Open weekends 11:00 A.M. – 5:00 P.M., other times by appointment
(705) 726-9198

John Poole Antiques:
John Poole, Hillsdale
Open Friday, Saturday, and Sunday
10:00 A.M. – 5:00 P.M., with extended summer hours
Best to call ahead (705) 835-3726

6

Black Shutter Antiques

Protection from Reproductions

Lawrence and Jean Hartnell have specialized in glass and china since opening Black Shutter Antiques in 1980. Soon after she and Lawrence were married, Jean discovered an 1880 Mary Gregory decanter that belonged to the Hartnell family. Lawrence began doing research on Mary Gregory glass, which stretched to research on other types of old glass, and for the Hartnells, the research has never ended.

Custard, cranberry, vaseline, carnival, opalescent, pressed—glass, glass, and more glass. Not only was glass made in a vast array of types and patterns, but it was also made in many countries. The subject of antique glass is a complicated one, and to add to the complexity, many old patterns and styles of both glass and china are being reproduced today. The novice collector must be wary.

So many pressed-glass patterns have been duplicated that a book is being written on the subject of reproductions alone. For example, in 1880 a company named the Cambridge Glass Co., in Cambridge, Ohio, began making clear and coloured pressed glass.

Surprise! Although often hard to distinguish, these are all reproductions.

Today, in that same town Mosser Glass is replicating the original patterns but in smaller sizes. Outside Pittsburgh, Pennsylvania, is a company which bought the moulds from the old Westmoreland Glass Co. and is remaking their pressed-glass patterns.

Neither of these modern pressed-glass manufacturers is trying to fool anyone, explains Lawrence. They are simply creating affordable pieces of glass for those who like the look of the old but can't afford authentic antiques. The trouble is, if you don't know the difference between the old and the new, you could purchase the new pieces at a flea market or auction sale for many times their value.

Lawrence divides glass and china reproductions into three categories. Exact copies he calls *reproductions*. *Look-alikes* meet the general description of the original, but are not exact. *Fantasy pieces* were not produced originally, but today are made by copying a certain pattern or technique.

Pieces of Nippon china are being reproduced today and marked "Handpainted Nippon." Look-alikes of Fiesta ware are being made, but the colours differ from those of the old Fiesta. The Fenton company is still making carnival glass, but the new pieces have the word *Fenton* embossed on the bottom. Blue willow china has been made in twenty different countries for the last two hundred years. New blue willow found in Canada is often marked with the English Burgess & Leigh mark. This company also reproduces ironstone.

The firm which imports the greatest number of reproductions, look-alikes, and fantasy pieces is the A.A. Importing Company Inc., in St. Louis, Missouri. A browse through their catalogue can be very enlightening. A monthly newsletter called *The Antique and Collectors Reproduction News*, P.O. Box 71174, Clive, Iowa, 50325, keeps Jean and Lawrence up to date on the latest imitations.

A marvellous profusion of Mary Gregory and cranberry glass.

In an effort to help their customers through the antiques maze, the Hartnells also sell reference books on all antique subjects. Specialist dealers will probably recognize reproductions immediately, but for the beginning collector, good reference material may be the best investment to make.

Black Shutter Antiques:
Lawrence and Jean Hartnell
Northeast of Stayner on County Road 7
Open most weekends
(705) 428-2116

A monthly newsletter called *The Antique and Collectors Reproduction News*, P.O. Box 71174, Clive, Iowa, 50325, keeps Jean and Lawrence up to date on the latest imitations. Out-of-print books on antiques are often recommended in this publication, and you can find copies of these books through:
Black Shutter Antiques, Box 670, Stayner, Ontario, L0M 1S0, or
Bakerosa Books and Collectibles, 188 Deer Park Circle, London, Ontario, N6H 3C1.

7

Blue House Antiques

Nostalgia—Remembering When

Is it possible that the urge to collect stems from a basic human need? Bob Charlton and wife Agnes have been collecting something or other since 1974—Persian rugs, Nippon china, furniture, nostalgia…. They opened Blue House Antiques eight years ago because their collection of toys and nostalgia had become too large: in order to keep buying they had to start selling.

When you buy nostalgia you are buying old forms of advertising—someone's effort to sell something. The field is so large that most nostalgia collectors like to narrow their focus to a specific area. Your chosen theme might be a subject—anything with pictures of cats on it, perhaps—or a type—maybe Canadian baking powder tins—or a brand, how about B.A. petroleum advertising?

Following the changing logos of a company can help you to date the items in your collection. As companies are bought and sold and amalgamated, the company's name and/or trademark evolves. With well-known companies, it's easy to discover the dates of these changes. Noting this evolution by studying the advertising of just one company can be a good learning experience for future dating of other nostalgia items.

The collector of early tins can trace the development of the process of tin decoration. The earliest are hand-painted, later ones are partially stencilled, with a paper label, and lithographing directly on the tin became popular in the 1890s. A tin can also be dated by the style of the picture on it—the clothes people are wearing, the cars they are driving, and other period details. The two major Canadian tin manufacturers were the Thos. Davidson Mfg. Co. Limited in Montreal and the Macdonald Co. Limited in Toronto. Since most tins carry the trademark of the maker, knowing the histories of these two companies is a good method of dating Canadian tins.

When buying any nostalgia, condition is always the most important consideration, but the colour of the graphics and the rarity of the item are also factors to consider. For example, a commemorative tin for a certain event is more interesting and will be more valuable than one made continuously over several years.

Speaking of tins, do you remember when you could buy sixteen ounces of peanut butter in a tin pail with a handle for twenty-five cents? Do you remember storing your marbles in it or taking it to the beach? Do you remember that as the years passed the price remained the same but the tin got smaller? (Probably your mother remembers this part.) Remember when cigarettes were sold in tin boxes called "flat fifties"?

And what about that urge to collect? Is it really a human necessity?

Bob's definitive answer is…perhaps. Since the beginning of time people have been hunters and gatherers. We no longer have to collect food or fuel for survival, but we still must satisfy the human need to find and store things. How do we do that? By finding and storing tins, furniture, dolls, toys—anything you'd like to imagine. At Blue House Antiques you'll discover a gathering of country items, furniture from 1840 to 1900, quilts, baskets, toys, nostalgia….

Remember when?

Blue House Antiques:
Bob and Agnes Charlton
North of Stayner on Highway 26
Open Thursday to Monday 10:00 A.M. – 5:00 P.M.
(705) 428-6943

ABOVE: Beware: collecting tins can become an obsession.
FACING PAGE: Bob's great toys

8

Art Glass Studio and Antiques
Soaring Eagle Publications

From the tranquillity of their shop beside the Thornbury mill pond, Cliff Golas and Connie Wills try to promote the antique business in any way they can. Twenty years ago, Cliff, self-described die-hard entrepreneur who grew up in the historic New Bedford area of Massachusetts, began buying, restoring and selling antique stoves. After a while this started to feel like a very heavy way to make a living. Then Cliff met Connie, who had lived on the mill pond since 1968. Together they opened the Art Glass Studio and Antiques shop eight years ago.

Cliff is a stained-glass artist, but his association with Connie has diverted his attention somewhat to early Canadian country furniture in pine and cherry. Although the couple don't specialize in antique art glass, they are intrigued by unusual antique accessory items and objects of art.

And what about Soaring Eagle Publications? Cliff and Connie have invested in some high-tech equipment, and four times a year they publish the *Georgian Antique Digest*, which is distributed throughout the southern Georgian Bay area. It's a small magazine catering to antique collectors. It carries informative articles about every facet of antiquity, and advertisers sell antiques and items related to antiques. You can pick up a free copy in any of thirty-five shops.

Why would two antique dealers want to get into the publishing business? When Cliff and Connie opened their business they began looking for local places to advertise. Finding nothing to suit their

ABOVE: Empire-styled butler's desk in cherry and figured maple.
RIGHT: Georgian Antique Digest staff could store their refreshments in this Globe ice-box from Boston.
FACING PAGE: Home of Art Glass Studio and Antiques, and the Georgian Antique Digest.

specific needs, in 1989 they came up with the idea of the digest.

Connie and Cliff believe that keeping a "quality mentality" is essential in the business, and to that end, they strive for quality in the digest and quality in what they sell. What are their criteria for quality? Pieces that require no more than ten percent restoration; pieces that retain their original finish are even better.

In this serene little town on the shores of Georgian Bay, an eagle soars, and for Cliff and Connie it's onward and upward.

Art Glass Studio and Antiques and Soaring Eagle Publications:
Cliff Golas and Connie Wills
22 Louisa Street East, Thornbury
(519) 599-5017

For a subscription to the digest, write:
Soaring Eagle Publications, 22 Louisa Street East, Thornbury, Ontario, N0H 2P0

9

The Bruce Beckons
From Log Cabin to Antique Dealer

At The Bruce Beckons, the coffee pot is always on. Over coffee, Gayle Thomas explains that she used to be a schoolteacher. One day, fifteen years ago, she was tempted by a real estate advertisement for a cedar log cabin on the Bruce Peninsula. Knowing nothing of the mysterious world of antiques she was about to be drawn into, she called her friend Edna Gibbons. The two of them drove up and down the concession road searching for the log home, but they couldn't find it. No wonder—when they finally hit the right house, they found that, like many other original log dwellings, the building had been faced with board and then insulbrick. Inside, the logs had been plastered over and then wallpapered. Undaunted by the huge restoration task ahead of them, Gayle and Edna bought the cedar log house.

When the project was completed, the log cabin seemed to cry out for period furnishings. Finding a surfeit of pieces they liked, the two decided to open an antique shop. Though Edna later tired of the

ABOVE: A hideaway full of treasures.
FACING PAGE: Gayle's smalls decorate the pre-Confederation cabin, a poker's paradise.

experience, Gayle discovered something about herself—she was an antique dealer.

Now Gayle says she can't imagine a more positive way of life. The excitement is in the find, of course, and the most incredible thing for Gayle is that after all these years she still comes across things she's never seen before.

Along with pine furniture, Gayle specializes in unique "smalls," and does most of her buying in Quebec. She enjoys the excitement of the "dealer only" auctions and "picks" regularly held in that province—especially as a lone woman. In Quebec this business is still primarily a man's game.

Butter work tables, wooden bird cages, a flat for eggs marked "Humpty Dumpty" and patented in 1886: Gayle buys such treasures and cleans them up carefully so that her customers can also appreciate their charm. She finds Quebec decoys interesting and less expensive than Ontario birds, since most of the Quebec carvers remain undocumented. Wooden washing machines, dye cabinets, sleighs, candle boxes, all kinds of wooden totes—including a lunch bucket from a Newfoundland trawler, and she recalls a wooden marble game marked with a patent date of 1882 that fascinated her so much she played with it all night. Like the log cabin, the aura of these things, the riddles they present, continues to fascinate.

The life of an antique dealer suits Gayle perfectly. That's why the coffee pot is always on at The Bruce Beckons.

The Bruce Beckons:
Gayle Thomas
North of Wiarton on Highway 6, turn right on Concession 4 and 5
Open weekends February 1 to December 31, Thursday to Sunday and holiday Mondays 10:00 A.M. – 6:00 P.M. during July and August
Shop (519) 534-1256, home (519) 534-3669

10

J & B Antiques

Influences on Ontario Country Furniture

"Cupboards are my passion," says Jim Phillips of J & B Antiques in Kincardine. His Great-Aunt Vera Lee had an antique store in Greenbank, and Jim remembers playing hide-and-seek in the armoires when he was growing up.

Jim began his own hunt for antiques by scouring the countryside for antique cars. "Of course I bought a good table or a cupboard if I saw one," he says with a chuckle. Gradually his interest shifted from cars to pre-Confederation country furniture. He's operated his shop on the shores of Lake Huron for twelve years.

Like most country furniture dealers, he has a particular liking for pieces from his own area—Bruce and Huron county pieces. Jim finds that these counties are an interesting study in influences.

Understanding how settlement patterns inspired Canadian cabinetmakers is the most important ingredient when studying our unique and varied furniture styles. This country was settled by people from various backgrounds. The majority came from the British Isles (the Scots, Irish, English, and Welsh), from France, from Germany, or were Loyalists from the United States who brought with them a whole history of European influences of their own. It was settled too by pockets of other nationalities, but all these pioneers had two things in common: they came with a dream and with a memory.

These people brought with them some knowledge of the furniture styles and traditions from their native countries, and as neighbour visited neighbour, as cabinetmaker taught apprentice, as one settlement mingled with another in this new country, they naturally influenced each other. Taste knows no social or ethnic barriers.

Bruce and Huron counties were settled predominantly by Scottish, German and Irish people. Look at the names of the towns: Kincardine, Kintail,

30

ABOVE: Notice the lozenge door panels and picture frame moulding which detail this early 19th-century Quebec cupboard in the centre of the picture. The pre-1840 cherry blanket chest to the left is signed Lundy's Lane, U.C. *(from Niagara Peninsula, Upper Canada). FACING PAGE: A glimpse inside J & B Antiques.*

Kinlough, Kinloss, Dungannon—obviously Scottish. Just to the east we have Hanover, Neustadt, and Carlsruhe—definitely German. The Irish settled around Walkerton and gave names to Tara and Dublin and others. The furniture that resulted has a definite German style, but with the added flair of raised panels and mullions not seen in Waterloo County German furniture of the same period. Travelling the countryside, knocking on doors and looking at antiques, has taught Jim that each area has its own unique "look" which can be traced back to the settlement of that area.

Jim likes to take pictures of the pieces he buys before he refinishes them. Before-and-after pictures show the customer exactly what repairs were done. Common repairs—replacing missing pieces of cornices, legging-out tables, or replacing backboards—are acceptable to most people.

Jim's son Aaron has been involved in the business since he was a wee lad. Now the two work together during Aaron's university breaks, carrying on a family tradition that started with Great-Aunt Vera Lee and that shows no sign of ending.

J & B Antiques:
Jim and Aaron Phillips
93 Goderich Street, Kincardine
Best to call ahead (519) 396-8261

SOUTH-WESTERN ONTARIO

Architectural finds from Artefacts in St. Jacobs.

11

John Forbes Antiques

Hooked on Pottery

Imagine the soothing sound of the potter's wheel as it turns, rendering a simple lump of clay, the earth we walk on, into something beautiful. Now think about discovering pieces of pottery that were hand-made by the earliest potters working in Ontario.

If this appeals, then you have something in common with John Forbes. John got hooked on pottery in 1975, the same year he became an antique dealer. In upper New York state that year, he found the earliest documented piece of Canadian pottery yet discovered. This brown-glazed, lidded pot is decorated with St. Ambros, the patron saint of beekeepers, suggesting that it was probably used for honey. The piece is signed by a Mennonite: "Jacob Boch, Waterloo, September 17th, 1825, Upper Canada."

Today John and wife Vikki live in a stone home just on the edge of Mennonite country. John continues to have a special fascination with early Ontario pottery, but he also sells pre-1850 Canadian and American painted country furniture and accessories.

The earliest Ontario pottery pieces, referred to as earthenware, came in two types: *redware* if made from red clay and *buff earthenware* if buff clay was used. The first home-potters or farmer-potters were cut off from civilization, and they laboured under many restrictions. Their ovens produced low firing temperatures, but they were still able to make practical pieces—pie plates, vases, cups and saucers, flowerpots, honey and tobacco jars—with a decorative flair. Because they used such low firing temperatures, they had the freedom to be creative, experimenting with colour and using such things as metal oxide splatters and freehand decorations to ornament their wares. Some pieces, like the Boch honey jar, have applied designs which were first made in moulds.

Collectors learn to recognize specific potter's pieces. William Eby of Conestogo placed a large cherry design on his pieces, while a potter named Bierenstihl, in Bridgeport, was able to achieve an

interesting purple glaze that retains its vibrancy today. Other collectable potters include Cyrus Eby of Markham, James Bailey from Bowmanville, Xavier Boehler in New Hamburg, and the Brownscombes, who travelled around the province, to name just a few.

By 1850, in Canada, independent earthenware potters were being replaced by pottery factories. These factories used much hotter furnaces and were thus able to fire *stoneware,* a very hard and durable pottery made from grey clay. These pieces were purely utilitarian—crocks and jugs and the like—and were ornamented more simply. The piece was fired, a simple freehand design—a bird, a fern, or a flower—was painted on, and then it was fired again. Called *slip decorations,* these designs were usually done in cobalt blue. Stoneware was often marked with the maker's name. Morton in Brantford, Skinner in Picton, and Eberhardt in Toronto were just a few of the larger Canadian pottery producers.

When we remember that the Dead Sea Scrolls were discovered well protected in pottery jars, it's not hard to understand our natural fascination with the quiet turn of the potter's wheel.

John Forbes Antiques:
Arkell, east of Guelph
By appointment
(519) 824-1842

Favourite references:
Early Ontario Potters, David L. Newlands
Early Canadian Pottery, Donald Webster

Visit the pottery collection at the Royal Ontario Museum in Toronto.

Examples of some of Ontario's earliest potters' work lean against the plate rails and decorate the shelves of this Scottish-influenced open dish dresser of the same period (1825–1850).

12

Patricia Korte Antiques

The Lure of the Decoy

Canvasback decoy by Isaiah Brown, Port Rowan, Ontario, circa 1900.

This country must have seemed spacious, wild, and awesomely beautiful when first viewed by white men. With its multitude of lakes and rivers it was home to abundant indigenous waterfowl, at least thirty-three different species. The native people hunted these birds, attracting them with rough decoys made of skins or fashioned from woven rushes and grass. European hunters progressed to carved lures, some of these carvers were true folk artists. Today their decoys attract not wildfowl, but also collectors, like Don and Patricia Korte.

Don and Patricia Korte opened Patricia Korte Antiques in 1976. Don Korte had been an English professor at the University of Guelph, but the world of historical objects began to invite him to stray. "I wanted to be able to touch and feel things, rather than dealing in abstract theories," he explains.

The Kortes sell country furniture and accessories, but in the last few years they have found themselves more and more attracted to the haunting forms of

On the right, a bluebill decoy by Bud Tully, Peterborough, Ontario, circa 1950, and on the left, a redhead by Tom Dalton, Hamilton, Ontario, circa 1870.

decoys fashioned by Ontario carvers. This growing interest is not hard to understand. Don's father worked for Louis Tiffany in the 1920s, sculpting marble and bronze, and Don's hobby is wood-carving, so it seemed a natural progression to sell decoys.

Don and Patricia feel strongly that study is paramount to the would-be collector, and to aid their customers in learning more, they sell all the Ontario decoy publications.

The birds the Kortes handle are authentic working decoys, researched and documented. The best decoys are original in all aspects. Paint is very important to the collector, as is form. Look at the tail and wing treatments, the position of the head, the naturalness of the bird. Does it look like it could fly away? Would it fool another bird? Weights, keels, buoyancy holes, whether a bird is hollow or solid, all are details decoy enthusiasts look for.

Collectors are lucky that Ontario decoys are such a well-documented subject. Identification of the carver is very important when assessing the value of the bird. The Kortes suggest that would-be decoy buyers ask the seller to guarantee the identity of the carver by writing his name on the receipt. Interestingly, decoys were often signed by their owners, not their carvers.

The carvers, folk artists in their own right, often have absorbing stories and are fascinating to research. Tom Dalton, for instance, an early carver from the Hamilton area, just disappeared; no one knows what happened to him. David Simandl of Chatham began carving birds after he lost both his legs in the Second World War. J.R. Wells, a Toronto decoy carver who was also a boatbuilder, is known to have carved only about thirty birds in his whole lifetime. The Nicholses from Smiths Falls passed on their carving tradition from generation to generation, and a little north of there, in Carleton Place, C. Morphy used old telephone poles to fashion his birds.

In 1866 sportsman and naturalist Major W. Ross King wrote that "a country like Canada, boasting a far larger extent of lake and river than any other under the sun, will be readily supposed to be inferior to none in the abundance and variety of its waterfowl." So, too, in its collectable decoys.

A selection of old Ontario decoys which used to attract waterfowl and now attract collectors.

Patricia Korte Antiques:
Patricia and Don Korte
Cambridge (Hespeler)
By appointment
(519) 658-2727

Favourite references:
Decoying, Barney Crandell
Decoys of the Thousand Islands, Jim Stewart and Larry Lunman
Ontario Decoys I and II, B. Gates
Decoys of Southwestern Ontario, P. Brisco
Traditions in Wood, P. Fleming

13

Artefacts

A Race with the Wrecking Ball

Scott Little and Chris Blott recycle early buildings, "buildings that would otherwise become fodder for the bulldozer," they explain, and to do this, they often find themselves in a race with the wrecking ball.

How did they get into this business? When Scott, who worked for the province of Ontario on heritage restoration projects, bought his own old house and began to restore it, he found himself searching for suitable parts. One day he noticed a block of nine houses scheduled to be destroyed. Peering through the windows, he saw historically interesting mantels, mouldings, and newel posts. He approached the wrecker about the possibility of salvaging some of these items, but the wrecker refused even to talk to him, so the next day Scott stood sadly on the sidewalk, watching as the row of houses, along with their vintage interiors, came tumbling down.

That was six years ago. Since then he and Chris have sprinted around the countryside saving every architectural object they can from destruction. Their shop, Artefacts, carries an ever-changing stock of indoor and outdoor architectural details: front entrances and interior doors, newel posts and railings, fireplace mantels, you name it.

Chris knows his hardware. Show him your front-door lock and he can tell you the age of your house, perhaps even its location. Scott was once an architectural purist, but he has moved a long way from those roots, and he and Chris now advocate doing whatever you want architecturally with periods and styles, as long as what you create is visually compatible with its surroundings.

They have done some interesting things over the years: turned a confessional into bookshelves, an altar into a shop counter, a gable end into a receptionist's

ABOVE: Salvaged from places past, architectural gems are here in the rough or unfinished.
FACING PAGE: An architectural junkie's paradise—be cautious of addition.

table, the list goes on and on. They are open to any suggestions. If you want restoration items for an old house, they'll help you find them. If you have an idea which incorporates architectural pieces, Scott and Chris will try to help you realize it. If you don't have an idea but want to have fun with something old and unique, they'll help you do that too. To that end, a stained-glass artisan works in the shop with them. If you accept the fact that a door does not merely have to function as a door, then there is no end to the possibilities.

Why are architectural antiques so popular? It's probably because not only do these original pieces continue to outshine new pieces in terms of the cost, but their patina and age create an aura in your home that nothing new could ever match.

If you can't save the whole house, at least you can preserve its parts. In the contest with the crane, Scott and Chris always try to win.

Artefacts:
Scott Little and Chris Blott
St. Jacobs
Saturdays 10:00 A.M. – 5:00 P.M., Sundays 1:00 P.M. – 5:00 P.M., weekdays by chance
(519) 664-3760

St. Jacobs is an attractive Mennonite village with several other unique shops.

14

Henry Dobson Antiques Ltd.
Elegance in the Provinces

Each antiquarian's journey takes different turns. For Henry and Barbara Dobson the long and demanding pursuit of their dream has led from turkey farming to an elegant Victorian hotel. Their goal? To find the finest of Canada's provincial heritage in furniture. Henry and Barbara are experts in this field.

Though many point to Canada's centennial year as the antique awakening, Henry Dobson claims that the real beginnings of excitement about our material heritage happened in the 1950s, when pine furniture, first discovered in barns and attics, was hauled out and stripped down inside and out. Henry and his first wife took up turkey farming after the war, and caught up in the excitement of rural life, furnished their home with antiques. In 1957 Henry left the turkeys and opened Henry Dobson Antiques.

Today Henry believes that design makes a piece of furniture, not the wood it is made of or the way it is

painted. This love of design has led Henry and Barbara in enthusiastic pursuit of the best of Canada's "provincial heritage," wherever it might be hiding. They have tried to discover those facets of Canadian material development that typify the best of taste in this country. In 1982 they put together an exhibition entitled "A Provincial Elegance" to showcase some of the finer pieces housed in private collections across the country.

Henry cites the French-Canadian armchair *à la Capucine* pictured in Jean Palardy's book, *The Early Furniture of French Canada*, as an example of such furniture. Simple yet elegant, it is a design unique to Canada, not copied from the provinces of France. Tall-case clocks and chandeliers made in this country from 1780 to 1830 are unequalled anywhere, in Henry's opinion.

Our earliest settled areas, the Maritimes and Quebec, are where the best and the finest Canadian furniture was produced. Unfortunately, many of the labels on this fine furniture were torn off as pieces were sold to the United States by the boxcar load, but cabinetmakers such as Thomas Nisbet (1750–1851) of Saint John, New Brunswick, built distinctive pieces that can be recognized and retrieved. It's never too late to reclaim your background or your heritage.

Henry and Barbara suggest building up a library of antique reference books and using that library extensively. Understand how our material heritage fits into the larger picture of world furniture styles. Acknowledge Canada's history—a history tied intricately to that of a very powerful and influential southern neighbour. Visit museums everywhere you go. Examine, criticize, discuss, and read. The joy is in the discovery. You must be prepared to see something

This Canadian Regency-style card table is from Quebec City, 1810–1820. Above hangs a high-relief wood carving attributed to the Baillargés, a family of Quebec carvers.

A Quebec tole chandelier from the Leclercville church steals the spotlight from the many other priceless treasures offered for sale here.

wonderful in the most unexpected places—a Nisbet sofa in a barn in Maine? Henry has seen that, and he prepared himself for this experience by doing his homework first.

Henry Dobson Antiques Ltd. is in Plattsville, housed in The Albion, an 1875 hotel which has been the Dobson home for over twenty years, and which Barbara now runs as a bed-and-breakfast. The rooms are furnished in the finest of antiques. You can place your clothes in a curly maple and mahogany chest of drawers from Canada's Maritimes, nestle down to sleep in an early-1800s American Sheraton canopy bed, and let your dream of early provincial elegance begin.

Henry Dobson Antiques Ltd.:
Henry and Barbara Dobson
Plattsville
Saturdays 10:00 A.M. – 5:00 P.M.
Sundays 1:00 P.M. – 5:00 P.M.
Other times by appointment
(519) 684-7434

Recommended places to visit:
Uniacke House in Windsor, Nova Scotia, to view well-labelled fine furniture.
Sigmund Samuel Canadiana Gallery of the Royal Ontario Museum, Toronto. (The gallery is at a separate location south of the museum on University Avenue.)

15

Douglas Stocks Antiques
Functional Antiquing

As a little boy in England, Douglas Stocks used to dig in his backyard to find pottery shards and then try to fit them together. He wanted to be an archaeologist when he grew up. Instead, he studied fine art and became a teacher, but the desire to find beautiful things and to try to understand them stayed with him.

Later, living in Canada, he began to buy antiques. In 1974 he started selling when his own collection outgrew his available space. He just couldn't stop digging for more! It's surprising how many antique dealers fell into the business this way.

Remembering his art training, when judging antique furniture Douglas keeps uppermost in his mind the knowledge that "form follows function." This was what that long-ago cabinetmaker knew when he began building a piece of furniture. This is what Douglas's customers have in their minds today as they search for just the right piece. It is a maxim that influ-

ences what Douglas sells: country and formal furniture, Canadian, American and European in origin; and large accessory pieces such as mirrors, rugs, and chandeliers—functional things.

Douglas judges whether formal furniture is functional first by looking at the proportions and overall form. He then examines how the cabinetmaker built the decorative elements onto that form. Do these decorative elements please the eye? Do they lighten the overall size? Finally he looks at the woods chosen, the originality of the finish, and the natural patina of the wood.

First find your piece, then grow to understand it through an analysis of its history and the culture from which it came. In Canada this can be an intriguing study, since this is a country complicated by several nationalities and converging styles. Our early country cabinetmakers had many influences working on them, including a knowledge of formal styles, and this pleni-

ABOVE AND FACING PAGE: This large shop of both formal and country antiques in original paints and refinished woods offers something for everyone's taste.

tude of ideas enriched our antique furniture. It makes the discovery and the eventual understanding of each piece you find all the more pleasurable.

Douglas's home, a large "Scottish baronial" stone house built in the 1850s, is the perfect education in influences. It was designed and built by a Scottish architect. The front of this house is formal, with twelve-foot ceilings, the back has lower ceilings and a definite country or provincial feel. Each of the front rooms is vented with a grate over the door. This unique venting design is French. How did this French design find its way into a home built by a Scotsman? A little study of Scottish history reveals the ancient ties that have long connected Scotland and France, and the influence that each has had on the other.

But these influences are so subtle and complex, how can anyone learn to really understand antique furniture? Make it fun, says Douglas. Like the food you eat, the objects around you should give you pleasure. Find pieces that attract you. Live with them and grow to understand them individually, without worrying about sticking to one period or style. You can appreciate pecan pie and a slice of rye bread at the same time, you can eat them at the same meal, just as you can mix periods and styles effectively in the same room.

Looking for antiques is, for Douglas, like being a child again, digging for the most attractive pottery shards with the goal of uncovering something wonderful.

Douglas Stocks Antiques:
On Highway 24A north of Paris
Open weekends 12:00 P.M. – 5:00 P.M. or by appointment
Shop (519) 442-7500, Home (519) 442-7007

43

16

Jonny's Antiques Ltd.
A Sleigh on the Roof

A visit to Jonny's in Shakespeare is a midsummer night's dream for antique lovers. His stock fills two houses and two large stores and spreads into the old Shakespeare firehall and a shed next door to the main store. The visitor to his shop also gets a walking tour of the picturesque Ontario hamlet named after England's most famous poet and playwright.

Jonny Kalisch began his career as an antique dealer on Wellesley Street in Toronto over thirty years ago. He placed a sleigh on his roof to attract attention.

Imagine having oolong tea with this Oriental screen as a backdrop.

Jonny says he found the little town of Shakespeare by accident, and he swears that it spoke to him. In 1970 he and his partner, James Bisback, left the city to establish their business in Shakespeare, and they have never looked back.

The sleigh was moved to its new home on the roof of the main store. After the deterioration of several sleighs, a weathervane was specially made for the roof, adorned with a sleigh that can brave the elements. But Jonny really doesn't need a sleigh on his roof to attract attention anymore; he has plenty of other things, including twin houses, cream with green trim, to draw customers. The houses are so unique that people just can't help stopping to take a picture of them.

The exclusive porcelain room at Jonny's Antiques

And Jonny has inventory—inventory covering several buildings and three centuries. The main store houses a dazzling display of porcelain and glass, all researched and identified. James is an expert on the subject of porcelain.

The furniture store has a broad range of formal and country furniture from many countries: Italy, France, England, Scotland, Wales, Germany, Denmark, the United States, and, of course, Canada. A random wander from the ground floor to the upstairs takes one through styles, periods, and countries—everything from an English canopy bed to a dazzling Quebec tramp-art sideboard to a huge Italian glass fountain that Jonny once took to a show but couldn't set up; it would have taken up his whole booth! And if you still haven't had your fill, meander down the street to the print store in one of the picturesque twin houses.

A midsummer night's dream and a winter's tale, as antique lovers like it—all in the little town of Shakespeare.

Jonny's Antiques Ltd.:
Jonny Kalisch and James Bisback
Shakespeare
Open daily 10:00 A.M. – 6:00 P.M.
(519) 625-8307

Also in Shakespeare:
Ten shops, including Agnes Gillespie Antiques and Glen Manor Galleries (both formerly Toronto dealers), Land and Ross Antiques, and Kathleen's Antiques, as well as a consortium of dealers under the banner of 2 Fraser Street.
In nearby Baden, visit:
J.C. Miller Antiques: (519) 634-8951

17

R. O'Hara Antiques
Beginning with a Blanket Box

The R. O'Hara antique shop spans three generations, and for nearly fifty years the shop's emphasis has been summed up in one word, *quality*. Quality in furniture, quality in glass, and quality in all the other small items that this shop offers.

In 1945 Ron O'Hara was working in his father's produce business. While he drove his pick-up truck from farm to farm, buying chickens for his father, he noticed discarded furniture in the barns and chicken coops, furniture that he felt had value. When asked,

the farmers were not only willing but anxious to sell. Very soon Ron had no more room for chickens; his truck was always full of antiques.

American dealers began to show up at his house in St. Mary's in station wagons with attached trailers. These dealers seemed to be prosperous. Antique

Front-row centre in the O'Hara garage is a pine open-dish cupboard with a Scottish influence and marquetry inlay work on the drawers.

O'Hara's makes pieces like this high-quality Mennonite corner cupboard its specialty.

dealing was in its infancy in Canada, so Ron and wife Rose decided to take a trip to the United States to learn more about running an antique business.

Ron and Rose have retired now, passing their knowledge of what constitutes quality on to their son, John, and their grandson, Mike. The Oxford dictionary defines *quality* as a "degree of excellence," and John believes that his major job as an antique dealer is to help his customers learn to recognize this degree of excellence in country furniture.

He starts by showing them something simple, like a blanket box. What gives this blanket box distinction? Examine its construction. Does it have an outside bracket base? Dovetailing? An interior till or document box? Cast-iron hinges or, better still, strap hinges? Examine the thickness of the wood and the width of the boards. Now step back and look at the box as a whole. How does it strike you? Does it have good size, proportion, and lines? What about original finish?

John likes paint that looks like the piece has lived, but he doesn't believe that paint can ever make up for lack of quality cabinetry. "Paint, to be great, must adorn a great piece," he says.

There is only one problem with being an antique dealer for the O'Haras. In order to make a living you have to sell things. Ron O'Hara is sure that if he had picked out each year's highest quality piece and kept it, today he'd make more selling that collection of prize pieces than he did throughout all his years in the antique business. Buy quality. It's the best guidance John can give today, and it's advice from his father, a man who has monitored the Canadian antique business for close to fifty years.

R. O'Hara Antiques:
615 Queen Street East, St. Marys
Open daily 8:00 A.M. – 5:00 P.M.
(519) 284-3887

18

Carol Telfer Antiques

How Old Is Your Textile?

A quilt represents many things: warmth, art, conservation, folk tradition.

Quilts first became popular in Europe during the Great Freeze in the fourteenth century. Even though today we have efficient central heating, quilts are still being pieced patiently together and lovingly quilted.

Carol Telfer specializes in quilts from the late 1700s to the 1940s, but also carries hooked rugs,

samplers, Victorian whites, cashmere and paisley shawls, and any other kind of needlework. She began in the antique business fifteen years ago with a booth at Harbourfront Market in Toronto. She's had shops in several locations since, and she now works out of her Stratford home. Her love of quilts has never waned. She feels that learning to recognize the age of a quilt is the most important thing for a potential quilt-buyer, and, she says, it's easier than you might think.

Fabric styles and patterns have changed about every twenty years. Study enough antique quilts, and you will notice that popular fabrics are seen over and over again. You can tell the age of a quilt by identifying the fabrics and patterns. Visit museums that have extensive, well-labelled textile exhibits and you can learn more about dating fabrics.

Remember, however, that quilt fabrics were often recycled. Examine the individual pieces used and date the quilt by the latest fabric it contains. Carol recalls once selling a quilt that was made from materials that spanned fifty years.

A study of the history of fabric-making is interesting and informative for the would-be quilt buyer. Initially all fabrics were handspun and hand-

From 1880 to 1900 was the era of Victorian crazy quilts, such as the one on the right, trimmed with handmade lace.

48

woven. During the eighteenth century, the numerous steps involved in fabric-making—spinning, weaving, bleaching, and dyeing—were industrialized one by one. Cloth printing using first wooden and then copper blocks led to a revolutionary discovery in the 1780s—a method of continuous printing using rotating copper cylinders. Commercial fabrics could then be printed in long sheets.

Wholecloth quilts are those made from wide printed strips of fabric. These were quite popular in Europe in the early 1800s. Earlier quilts of the era were often larger since the beds were higher. Quilts made for poster-style beds had cut-out corners at one end to fit around the bottom posts. These help to date a quilt too.

Be cautious, warns Carol. There is some danger of buying a reproduction quilt. Cottons can be artificially aged with washing. A brand-new Amish-style quilt can be made to look just like an Amish quilt from the 1940s.

Once you have learned how to date quilts you are on your way as a collector. Establish your own personal parameters, appreciating the design and quality of workmanship that went into each quilt creation. See and touch as many quilts as you can. A visit to Carol Telfer Antiques is one way to begin your education.

The folk art tradition is strong in this circa 1820 Ontario quilt using blue and white calico prints.

Carol Telfer Antiques:
312 Cobourg Street, Stratford
By appointment
(519) 271-0941

Museums to visit:
The Shelburne Museum in Shelburne, Vermont (open mid-May to mid-October)
The Abby Aldrich Rockefeller Folk Art Center in Williamsburg, Virginia (open all year)

Books to Read:
America's Glorious Quilts, edited by Dennis Duke and Deborah Harding

The Romance of the Quilt in America, Carrie A. Hall and Rose G. Kretsinger

How do you wash an antique quilt?
Orvis Paste or Aunt Beth's Natural Fibre Shampoo, available through Aunt Beth's Quilt World, R.R. 2, Navan, Ontario, K4B 1H9.

19

Peter and Janis Bisback
The Desire to Preserve

How can the desire to preserve an old church lead one into the antique business?

In 1980 the white wooden Anglican church next door to Janis and Peter Bisback's home in Hensall went up for sale, and something inside the couple was touched by the thought of what could happen to the old building in the wrong hands. Long-time preservers of the past, they were further disturbed by the rumour that a potential buyer intended to chop the church up into apartments. In short order, they found themselves owning a church—a church that was uninsurable until they had designated a use for it. And that's how Peter and Janis decided to open an antique store.

Asked about their merchandise, Janis quickly answers, "Canadian." In fact, they deal mostly in Ontario items, including many local pieces. Peter and Janis don't remove paint, even overpaint. They sell things as they find them, believing that this is part of preservation. Even cleaning is done conservatively. What makes its way into their preserved church are things that they feel need to be kept just as they are— furniture, folk art, tools, and nostalgic items such as trade signs.

What is nostalgia? To Janis, it's a memory—a memory of the warmth of Grandma's knee, of the smell of her kitchen. Sometimes nostalgia is a longing for one's own childhood, for a time you want to believe was simpler and easier to define. Maybe nostalgia is a desire to preserve time, to keep it fixed forever.

Nostalgic items are things that people want to remember and to keep around them. They are items to decorate your home with, things that allow you to enjoy a pleasurable memory.

How do you buy nostalgic items? Nostalgically, of course. However, if you insist on being practical about it (an idea that is almost in conflict with the entire concept of nostalgia), then try to think about condition and rarity when you are making a purchase. The best of nostalgia is in perfect or near-perfect condition. Remember that nostalgia prices are established by supply and demand, and therefore they can fluctuate from area to area. American prices are not necessarily the same as Canadian, for the simple reason that Americans and Canadians have different memories.

Be careful: nostalgia is being reproduced. You can reproduce anything, explains Janis, even rust spots. Examine popular items such as Coca Cola advertising very carefully. Articles with an international focus are more likely to be remade, since they have a larger market.

Peter and Janis understand preservation. They believe in keeping things the way they are found. And they have a white church full of memories for you.

Peter and Janis Bisback:
88 Queen Street, Hensall
By chance or appointment
(519) 262-3505

Want to know more about nostalgia? Visit the quarterly Woodstock Nostalgiarama Show in Woodstock.

Facing page: A churchful of unique offerings.
Above: This 1877 former Anglican church holds the Bisbacks' preserved prizes.

20

Randy Plester Antiques

Ontario Oak—The Best You Can Buy

Randy Plester was carrying on a family tradition when he decided to become an antique dealer—his father was a wholesale antique buyer. In his teens, Randy put together an extensive collection of clocks. In 1974, when he decided to become an antique dealer, he sold this collection to finance the enterprise.

His shop in London carries antiques and collectables from 1860 to 1930, including primitive furniture, Depression furniture, Depression glass, nostalgia items, and his favourite, turn-of-the-century oak. There isn't much pine furniture in the London area, as the preference here has always been for a more formal look, often represented by oak.

Furniture now referred to as "turn-of-the-century oak" was also made in elm, ash and chestnut, and was mass-produced by mechanized means from 1885 to 1910. It has been quite collectable for several years. About fifty percent of turn-of-the-century oak pieces carry the manufacturer's label, either paper or burned on. Sometimes shipping labels are still attached too, which adds to the provenance.

When buying oak furniture keep in mind that the best quality is quarter-cut oak. "Quarter-cut" refers to the method of sawing. The oak log was first quartered lengthways, and then these quarters were sawn into boards. This created a very interesting wood grain as well as helping the oak to resist shrinking and warping. Of course, there was more waste when quarter-cutting oak, and it was time-consuming. These two factors made it a more expensive product. According to Randy, quarter-cut turn-of-the-century oak pieces sell for thirty to fifty percent more than similar pieces in other hardwoods.

Since people in London and the surrounding area liked more formal styles, oak furniture was very popular here, and there were many local manufacturers. Of these, the George McLacan Furniture Co. in Stratford manufactured the best quality. McLacan is the most collectable Canadian oak one can buy today. As well, there was the London Furniture Company, in business only a short time, and the Lucknow Table and Chair Company, which made pressbacks and round and square oak tables. The Owen Sound Furniture Company made good oak furniture, as did the Canadian Furniture Co. in Woodstock.

Ontario's oak furniture manufacturers were among the best in North America. Often there was more refinement in their styling than in that of their American counterparts. In fact, even American oak collectors prefer Canadian pieces, Randy says. Isn't that a pleasant discovery?

A Hamm and Nott oak icebox from Brantford, Ontario, circa 1900, at left, and a Krug drop-front desk in the arts and crafts styles of the 1920s.

Randy Plester Antiques:
311 Horton Street, London
Open Wednesday to Saturday 10:00 A.M. –
5:00 P.M. or call for an appointment
Shop (519) 434-4477, Home (519) 681-6349

Turn-of-the-century oak at its finest.

Uniquely designed side tables in oak.

21

Old London South Antiques

The Rare Pleasure of Figured Maple

B ird's-eye and tiger maple are two specialty woods that have an uncommon appeal to antique lovers. Many years ago Bill Heinsohn received a gift of a bird's-eye maple two-drawer lamp table from his aunt. Bill was hooked.

Fifteen years ago he opened Old London South Antiques, carrying a general line of Canadian fine furniture, porcelain and glass, toys and teddy bears, as well as Oriental pieces: porcelains, bronzes, ivories, and fans. John Nixon has been his partner in the business for the last several years.

Specialty maple pieces still capture Bill's attention, and he is always on the lookout for them. When settlers first came to this country, Bill relates, a dense forest spread from the United States into Southern Ontario, eastward from the Great Lakes. It was the bountiful, lush Carolinian forest, and it contained an incredible abundance of woods. Stretching as far as

BELOW: Bedtime for the teddies in this tiger maple bed, circa 1860, from Brantford, Ontario.
RIGHT: Butler's desk with Hepplewhite influence from New York state, circa 1810–1820.

the eye could see in every direction, the Carolinian forest was a cabinetmaker's dream come true.

One of the many hardwoods growing in the Carolinian forest was the sugar maple. Maple has a tendency to twist after it is milled, but, Bill explains, something unique happened with one out of about every thousand sugar maple trees. It twisted as it grew. This growth and twisting went on uninterrupted for over five hundred years, and the result was "figured wood"—bird's-eye maple and tiger maple.

Though they look so different, bird's-eye and tiger maple can come from the same tree. The difference is in the milling. Cut one way, this rare tree produces

Note the pronounced bird's-eye in this chest of drawers from Owen Sound, Ontario, circa 1840.

bird's-eye. Cut in the opposite direction, the resulting lumber is tiger. Prove this to yourself by looking at the side of a piece of furniture where the dots, or bird's eyes, show on the front. The side view will look striped, or tiger. Some areas produced different growth than others; Bill has found that pieces originating in the Owen Sound area have a particularly dense bird's-eye configuration.

A maple yielding wide bird's-eye or tiger lumber was hard to find one hundred and fifty years ago; probably impossible to find today. When you see a piece of antique furniture made of large figured maple boards, you are looking at an extremely rare item.

Old London South Antiques:
Bill Heinsohn and John Nixon
169 Wortley Road, London
Monday to Saturday 10:00 A.M. – 5:00 P.M. or by appointment
(519) 432-4041

22

The Pig 'n' Plow
From a Mystic Realm

Much of our material history might have been lost had it not been for those who began to collect and deal in antiques many years ago. Those early collectors of Canadiana had very little to go on except their love of the country and its historical objects, and their own good "eye."

In baseball, if you have a good eye you know when to swing the bat. In antiques, a good eye makes itself known by a certain chiming inside the head when you're looking at something great. Marjorie Sackrider Larmon thinks that one might be born with a good

The Sackrider homestead.

eye for antiques. She herself has had an abiding love of old things since the age of ten, and has been a dealer for forty-five years, selling antiques from her birthplace, the Sackrider homestead, for most of them. Here, Quaker resourcefulness and her own family's history dwell in every nook and hide in every cranny.

What Marjorie Larmon can't hide is her glee over antiques. When she shows you her fifty-one-inch, carved and painted cigar-store Indian, so real you could almost take the wooden tobacco he offers, and exclaims, "Isn't it wonderful!"—a carillon rings in your head, because wonderful he is indeed.

"I suppose it was my Pennsylvania Dutch father's inquisitive, resourceful nature, which I inherited, that fashioned my early interest in the mystic realm of folk art," Marjorie says. She began collecting what is now called "folk art" over thirty years ago, and back then people laughed at her "odd" choices. A hooked rug sporting a rooster, which she bought because it carried the year of her mother's birth, 1888, was the start of her rug collection. A quilt made by her great-grandmother, depicting early settlers gazing from their log cabin window at Indians hunting deer, is what kindled her interest in quilts.

Most dealers buy and sell what they value themselves. Today they are helped by scholarly documentation on many subjects, but when Canadian antique-collecting began, dealers and collectors had only their own instincts to rely on.

Admitting that she can get "testy" on the subject of quality, Marjorie would like to see Canadians learn more about their heritage and then guard that knowledge, and the best of those material objects which define it, for future generations to enjoy. Marjorie Larmon used her own history as her starting point and moved into antique-collecting from there. Once, many years ago, she asked her father if she could borrow $500 to buy an antique.

"Is it worth it?" he asked.

"It will be," she replied.

Marjorie knew then what many are just now learning: quality Canadiana isn't expensive—it's priceless.

The Pig 'n' Plow:
Marjorie Larmon
On Highway 59 east of Burgessville
Summer hours only
Please call ahead (519) 424-9997

ABOVE: A superbly furnished barn, home of the Pig 'n' Plow.
LEFT: Interior of the Sackrider barn cum antique shop.

23

Ruth Jones Antiques
Yesterday's Gas Lamps for Today

Lighting up our lives was accomplished in many ways during the nineteenth century. From candles to Betty lamps to gas lighting (where natural gas was available), from oil-burning lamps to electric light—that century saw great change in the way we staved off the winter darkness and lengthened our productive days into the evening hours.

Today Ruth Jones Antiques, established in St. Catharines in 1968, provides Canadians with light from a source that is antique yet practical. Ruth started the business with her late husband, Eric, a buyer for General Motors. "Eric was a frustrated salesman," Ruth laughs. When their son, Earl, joined Ruth in the business, he brought with him an interest in gas lighting. Earl learned the best method of converting brass gas lamps to electricity to make them usable in modern homes. Today the lamps come from sources all over North America, and Earl cleans and polishes them to perfection.

North Americans experienced gas lighting for the first time in 1817, when the city of Baltimore, Maryland, began to illuminate its streets with gas lamps. Toronto made gas lighting available in 1840, and by the 1850s mass production of gas lighting devices was in full swing.

Electricity put an end to gas lighting. The sale of electricity began as a private enterprise in the late 1880s, with individuals purchasing small electric generators in order to provide electricity for themselves and their neighbours. By 1900 cities were buying large generating systems, and the age of electricity had begun in earnest.

A selection of Ruth's finest glass and china.

At this point many gas fixtures and lamps were converted to electricity.

Two pieces of antiquity are encompassed in the gas lamp: the brass base and the glass shade. Ruth and Earl have a large inventory of both antique lamps and antique shades, allowing you to choose whatever shades you prefer to complement your polished brass fixture. It's easy to differentiate between a gas lamp and an early electric lamp, by the way. Just look for the stopcock on the lamp, which turned the gas flow on and off.

Earl has chandeliers, wall sconces, table lamps, student lamps, floor lamps—all the lighting you might need for your home. Ruth carries furniture and Victorian kitchen gadgets, and her specialty, fine glass and china.

There's plenty of light available in St. Catharines—rare and beautiful light.

Gas lamps, converted to electricity, glow over Ruth and Earl's antiques.

Ruth Jones Antiques:
Ruth and Earl Jones
69 Queenston Street, St. Catharines
Open Tuesday to Saturday
10:30 a.m. – 5:00 p.m.
(905) 685-5001

Recommended Reading:
American Lighting 1840–1940, Nadja Maril

24

Queenston Antiques

Clues About Early Rope Beds

Upper Canada (now Ontario) was first opened up for settlement and commerce by enterprising men and women from Great Britain. In the Niagara Peninsula, Sir Robert Hamilton Sr. was granted 22,000 acres around the town of Queenston. Mrs. Hamilton's Christian name, Catharine, was later bestowed on St. Catharines, just as the family's surname was given to the city of Hamilton. In 1807 they built an elegant red-brick house in Queenston for their son, Robert Hamilton Jr.

One hundred and fifty-three years later, Jonathan Kormos bought Robert Jr.'s house and began furnishing it with tall-case clocks and high-post beds—the Canadian equivalent of the type of fine furniture Jonathan's wife, Elizabeth, remembered from her home in England. In his quest for furnishings he did business with two antique dealers who were bed specialists. Both were happy to share their acquired knowledge with him, and when Jonathan Kormos opened Queenston Antiques he made rope beds his specialty.

Selling beds for thirty-four years has taught Jonathan Kormos a great deal about rope beds. The four bed rails of rope beds were joined to the four posts with a mortise-and-tenon joint, usually secured with a bolt. You can spot the very earliest Ontario rope beds because they didn't use bolts, relying simply on the roping to hold the joints together. Upper Canada's blacksmiths at that time had no way of threading a bolt, and although bedmakers could buy bolts from Europe or the United States, they usually didn't.

Jonathan dates Ontario rope beds by examining the rails. Square rails with holes for the ropes were usually made before 1835. Square rails with pegs to which the ropes were secured can be dated between 1830 and 1850. Around this time round rails began to replace square ones. Depending on the area, round-rail beds with rope holes were made between 1840 and 1860. Round rail beds with pegs may have been made as late as 1875. There were no rope beds constructed after that time. Cast-iron connectors that resemble horseshoes were used after 1875, and the modern steel double hook appeared at the turn of the century.

Canadian beds were handsome but plain. Carving was rarely done on a bed made in this country. Beds were custom-made, so antique beds are as variable in size as were the people who slept in them. Rope beds, however, are usually very short. In fact, the longest bed Jonathan has ever seen was only six feet long. These short beds must be modified to make them usable today. By replacing the side rails with longer ones and giving the customer the original rails to store, the modification for use can be made as minor as possible.

Jonathan has over two hundred and fifty rope beds in his inventory. This includes tall-post beds (both canopy and tester), low-post beds, under-eave beds, beds embellished with pineapples, acorns, cannonballs, bells, and tulips—in fact, every kind of bed you could imagine. He also sells Niagara Peninsula pieces, pieces in figured woods, and Quebec pieces.

Living as he does, in the historic red-brick house with the ghosts of the family that gave two Ontario cities their names, it's no wonder that for over a quarter of a century Jonathan's main preoccupation has been Canada's material history.

Queenston Antiques:
Jonathan Kormos
93 Queenston Street, Queenston
By appointment
(905) 262-4796

Note the intricate beehive turnings on the footposts of this 1790 Nova Scotia birch tester bed in original cherry colour.

25

Creighton House Antiques

Treasure Hunter

Jowe Creighton, a picker, wishes that there was a better word for what he does. He suggests "direct antique buyer," but confesses that what he really feels like is a "treasure hunter." What Jowe does—every day of the week from nine to five—is travel in his truck, knocking on doors and purchasing treasures.

It was Jowe's wife, Pauline, who got him interested in antiques. She had been going to auctions and buying before she met Jowe, and after they married, they found that the habit was progressive. They started out with small things, and their interests grew.

Jowe found that he had a tremendous desire to buy. It was the love of the goods themselves that drove him. These things were real, they were unique, and they had withstood the test of time. Somehow, he had to find a way to support this habit.

The excitement that comes with a great find has never left him. He recalls the first day he went picking—or treasure-hunting. He knocked on a door, and the people said, yes, they had some old things they'd like to sell. Jowe started up the stairs, and when he saw what was sitting on the landing he thought his heart would jump out of his body—an early Loyalist blanket box with a remarkable cut-out base and the original unblemished paint simulating a mahogany wood grain. Jowe still owns that first great find.

After several years of picking only in Canada, Jowe started treasure-hunting in the States. It wasn't that the pickings were better there, it was mainly that the winters were warmer. Looking through peoples' basements, barns and attics in the Canadian winter can be a mighty cold experience.

The eclectic finds of Jowe Creighton.

Jowe's pickings in front of Creighton House.

Treasure hunters are the first step in the preservation of antiques. They buy from people who don't care for their old stuff, who are, in fact, glad to be rid of it, to replace it with modern furniture and equipment. Treasure hunters save our material history from the woodstove and from wood rot. Jowe recalls knocking on the door of a house where two old bachelors lived. They'd be glad to sell him anything, they chuckled, since their house had been furnished from the local dump. Naturally, much of what they had was worthless, but Jowe did find a pearl in the sand—a fine pail stand in the original green paint, which the two old gents insisted was the worst thing they'd salvaged.

You can tell, talking to him, that Jowe likes the people he buys from. Some of them he visits often, not to buy, but because they're lonely and need the company.

His shop—oh yes, there is a shop: didn't I say he had to support his habit?— is an eclectic mixture of Canadiana, oak furniture, glass and china, even American Depression furniture. American Depression furniture was made cheaply during the Dirty Thirties. People bought it—and still buy it—for its function alone. Will it ever be collectable or have an antique value? Jowe doesn't think so, but who can predict the future market?

Imagine spending your life on a gigantic treasure hunt—no wonder Jowe's smile is a permanent fixture.

Creighton House Antiques:
Jowe Creighton
3791 Main Street, Jordan
Open Saturday and Sunday, 12:00 P.M. – 5:00 P.M.
(905) 562-4461

63

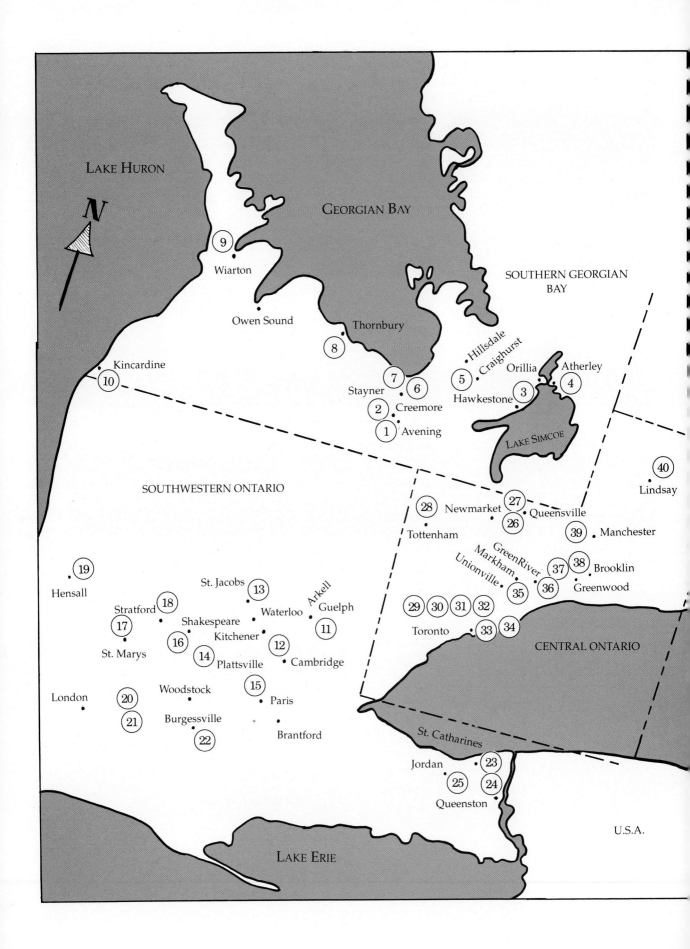

LAKE HURON

GEORGIAN BAY

SOUTHERN GEORGIAN BAY

⑨ Wiarton

Owen Sound

Thornbury

⑧

Hillsdale
Craighurst

⑦ ⑥
Stayner ⑤ Orillia Atherley
② Creemore ③ ④
① Avening Hawkestone

LAKE SIMCOE

Kincardine

⑩

SOUTHWESTERN ONTARIO

⑩ ㉗

⑳ Newmarket ㉗
㉖

Tottenham ㊴ Manchester

GreenRiver
Markham ㊲ ㊳ Brooklin
Unionville ㊱
⑲ ㉟ Greenwood
Hensall

St. Jacobs ⑬
Stratford ⑱ Arkell
Shakespeare Waterloo Guelph
⑰ ⑯ Kitchener ⑪
St. Marys ⑭ ⑫
Plattsville Cambridge

⑳ Woodstock ⑮
London ㉑ Paris

Burgessville Brantford
㉒

㉙ ㉚ ㉛ ㉜
Toronto ㉝ ㉞

CENTRAL ONTARIO

St. Catharines

Jordan ㉓
㉕ ㉔
Queenston

U.S.A.

LAKE ERIE

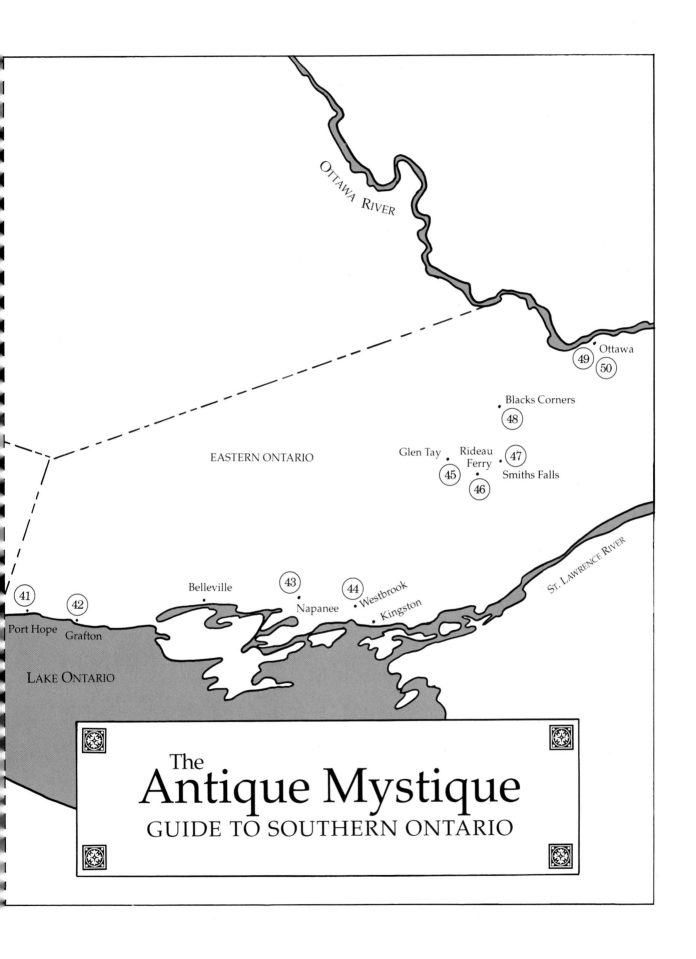

OTTAWA RIVER

49 • Ottawa
50

Blacks Corners
48

EASTERN ONTARIO

Glen Tay • Rideau
Ferry 47
45 • Smiths Falls
46

ST. LAWRENCE RIVER

43
Belleville 44 • Westbrook
• Napanee • Kingston

41
42
Port Hope Grafton

LAKE ONTARIO

The
Antique Mystique
GUIDE TO SOUTHERN ONTARIO

CENTRAL
ONTARIO

A selection of pieces from J.W. Humphries Antiques Ltd. in Lindsay.

26

Newmarket Century House Antiques
Kerosene Lighting

In these days of abundant artificial light, it's hard to imagine not having that commodity at the flick of a switch. But winter in Canada for our forebears was a very different prospect. When the sun set at four o'clock on a winter's day, light ended. Its not hard to understand why it was a Canadian who invented kerosene lamp fuel, an invention that led to an awesome variety of lamp designs.

Joanne and Gerry Bloxam of Newmarket Century House Antiques have long been fascinated by all those early lighting devices that burned kerosene. They set themselves the task of learning everything they could about kerosene lighting, and what started as a collection quickly grew into a business. First, the Bloxams sold lamps at shows, and then, in 1986, they opened their permanent shop on Main Street in Newmarket.

Joanne feels it's important to remember that people originally used kerosene lamps not just because they were practical, but to decorate their homes as well. The cost of them varied greatly, ranging from twenty-five cents to twenty-five dollars. "As with every antique, the best then is still the best today," says Joanne.

Lamps that stood on a table were called stand lamps. They date from the 1850s to the early 1900s. You can recognize early stand lamps since they were made in two pieces: a font, or reservoir for the oil, and a base, with a metal (usually brass) connector between the two. These early stand lamps have distinctive metal burners called lange burners. Later lamps used prong burners.

As lamp sales increased, a myriad of patterns were produced in clear and coloured glass, sometimes with as many as ten sizes in each pattern. Miniature lamps were also manufactured; they were used as night lights.

Today's most popular patterns, according to Joanne, are bull's-eye lamps in clear and green glass, and the princess feather lamp in cobalt blue. Watch out for reproductions, however. Joanne keeps a reproduction green bull's-eye finger lamp in the store so that she can put the original beside the reproduction to show customers how to spot the differences.

As well as stand lamps, many types of kerosene-burning hanging lamps were made. Hanging lamps made of cast iron reached their peak of popularity from the 1860s to the mid-1870s. Sometimes the cast iron was highlighted with green or gold paint. Most cast-iron lamps are marked with patent dates. The patent dates Joanne sees most often are 1868 and 1871.

Around 1880, brass and white-metal hanging lamps replaced cast iron in popularity. These were called fourteen-inch hanging lamps. They sported glass fonts and shades in cranberry, blue, pink opaline, and other fine coloured glass, and they were adorned with hanging glass prisms. They were sold until the turn of the century and can sometimes be dated by patent dates appearing on the motor which raises and lowers the lamp.

The Bloxams like to sell all their lamps with old chimneys and burners, though Joanne laments that old chimneys are getting harder and harder to find these days.

A variety of fourteen-inch hanging lamps which burn kerosene.

And now, are you wondering about that Canadian who invented kerosene and started all of this? His name was Dr. Abraham Gesner. Born in rural Nova Scotia, Dr. Gesner's hobby was geology, and he discovered kerosene by accident in 1846. Little did he know that he had initiated something not only radiant but practical, extending our hours of productivity and pleasure.

The Bloxams of Newmarket are keeping that kerosene radiance alive.

Newmarket Century House Antiques:
Joanne and Gerry Bloxam
78 Main Street South, Newmarket
Open Tuesday to Saturday 10:00 A.M. – 5:00 P.M.,
Sunday 10:00 A.M. – 3:00 P.M.
(905) 773-6355

Kerosene lighting is the specialty of Newmarket Century House Antiques.

Recommended Reading:
Oil Lamps, volumes I and II, Catherine Thuro

For a kerosene lamp experience, visit Black Creek Pioneer Village's Christmas by Lamplight on the first weekend in December. All lamps provided by Newmarket Century House Antiques. For information, call (416) 736-1733, ext. 404.

Do you know about the Historical Lighting Society of Canada? Contact Don Jewell, R.R. 6, Barrie, Ontario, L4M 5P5

27

The Cat's Meow
Collecting Smalls

"No one intends to go into the antique business," says Flo Lewis of The Cat's Meow. But when your husband's great-great-great-great-great-grandfather came from that famous family of master builders and cabinetmakers, the Doans of Sharon Temple fame; and when his mother and grandmother collected antiques; and when you, yourself, started collecting old things when you were a child, dragging stuff home from your grandfather's barn to decorate your room—well, somehow or other you end up in the antique business.

At Flo and Don's, the cats and the collectables spill out of and over the antique furniture. For antiquers it's the cat's meow, indeed. Flo describes their tastes and their wares as eclectic. They carry pine, cherry and butternut furniture from the nineteenth century,

RIGHT: These children's rockers are definitely "The Cat's Meow."
FACING PAGE: Baskets, boxes, and totes are among the many offerings of The Cat's Meow.

treenware (antique talk for any small item made of wood), metalware, baskets, and anything that strikes their fancy.

If you collect small items, explains Flo, then every shop has a bargain in it. It's the same thing at the big shows. If you know your "smalls" and your prices, you can always find good buys.

Flo particularly likes wooden cheese boxes, wooden totes, small wooden boxes, and small baskets. The little baskets are fun to look for and hard to find. She surmises that they were used for herb collecting, as small lunch baskets, or perhaps children's sewing baskets. When you're looking at baskets, examine the fine details in the way they were made. Look for features like hinges on baskets with lids. Note if special care was taken in attaching the handles. It is the detail work that shows the talent and ingenuity of the basket weaver. Baskets with colour, baskets with looped designs, baskets with sweetgrass: all such details add to the interest and value for the collector.

Back when her children were small, Flo started buying child-size rockers for them, and now she uses the excuse of future grandchildren to keep buying the scaled-down furniture.

Flo and Don of The Cat's Meow have been in the antique business for sixteen years. "Once you're into it, you can never get out," says Flo. "I think it's a disease."

The Cat's Meow:
Flo and Don Lewis
On County Road 12 just north of Queensville
A phone call ahead is recommended
(905) 478-1450

28

High House Antiques

The Romance of the Tester Bed

You dream of a weekend in a country house high atop a hill. After dark, you climb the stairs to the bedroom and clamber up into a canopied four-poster bed. Ahh…your personal retreat from the madding crowd. The private place where your future and your past meld, becoming one in your dreams.

It's no surprise to discover that the first antique purchased by Jane Stief, the owner of High House Antiques, was a bed. Little did Jane understand then the passionate grip that antiques were about to make on her future. Today she has been an antique dealer for over twenty years, specializing for the last seven in antique beds of every variety.

Certainly our ancestors understood the importance of the bedchamber, says Jane. Brides came to their marriage complete with their bed furnishings: linens, sheets, pillowcases, quilts, blankets, and coverlets—everything necessary to adorn their marriage bed and to keep the couple warm through the long cold nights. In the cramped quarters of log cabins the bed was often the only private place for a married couple—the only retreat from a very harsh world. And don't forget that the canopy bed style, around since the sixteenth century, was firmly ensconced in the minds of North American settlers as the bed of the upper classes.

Today, sentiment, romance and nostalgia thrive in the bedchamber, and mystery abounds. No antique bed more typifies this fantasy than the canopy or tester bed. If you want to feather your nest with the best, this is it. It is the best, according to Jane, first and foremost because of its form. If you stand back and look at any piece, be it a tester bed or a corner cupboard, and mentally strip away the carvings and trims, the form should sing to you. As writer Albert Sack explains it in *Fine Points of Furniture*, "Detail becomes important only when it is combined with successful design."

Warmth played a large part in the early design of beds. They had curtains and canopies. They had high feet and stood well off the floor. They were placed not against walls, but in the centre of rooms. There was one reason for all this—to avoid drafts. Headboards and footboards contributed to the warmth. Footboards were sometimes removed in the summertime to let the air circulate more freely, especially in the southern United States. Blanket rails were free-turning so that extra blankets could be

ABOVE: Ontario cherry high-post bed in the Empire style from Waterloo County, with added tester frame, circa 1840.
FACING PAGE: Beds galore at High House Antiques.

wrapped around them and unrolled as needed during the night.

Jane sells other country furnishings and accessories as well as beds. Like most dealers, she buys and sells what she personally appreciates the most. Her taste is for what she describes as "upper country," and what others call "high country." These are country furnishings tending towards formal design and workmanship.

In the end it doesn't really matter what type of bed or furnishings you choose, says Jane, as long as you surround yourself with things that are beautiful to you, things that are useful to you, and things that you love.

High House Antiques:
Jane Stief
Three miles north of Tottenham on the corner of Tecumseth 7th Line and Adjala– Tecumseth Town Line
Open 10:00 A.M. – 5:00 P.M. daily
A call ahead is recommended
(905) 936-4750

Recommended Reading:
Fine Points of Furniture, Albert Sack

Jane Stief holds six antique workshops per year. For "A Day in the Country" call High House Antiques.

29

R.G. Perkins and Son Antiques

The One-Hundred-Year Criterion

For thirty-two years an antique trade sign has stood above Yonge Street in Toronto. For thirty-two years the Perkinses, first Bob and now Sheldon, have been purveyors of quality Canadian country furniture and accessories at this location.

Bob Perkins's initiation into antiquity was in the early 1950s. Restoring furniture for a habitant museum in Chambly, Quebec, he found he liked the stuff.

Since the museum was low in funds, he took payment for his work in antiques. He got to know the woman who did the buying for the village and began to accompany her on antique-hunting trips. In 1957 he started picking on his own in Quebec and selling his finds to Toronto dealers. Four years later he moved to Ontario and opened his business. When Bob was looking for help in the early seventies, his son Sheldon applied for the job, and the present-day R.G. Perkins and Son antique firm was born.

To be an antique, Sheldon says, an article must be one hundred years old. There is no other criterion. It's not an antique if your grandmother got it for a wedding present in 1940.

The quickest way of dating furniture is to look at the nails that hold the piece together. Initially, nails were all handmade. Hand-forged nails are not uniform in length or thickness. But how do you recognize them if they're hammered into the furniture and you only have the nail head to look at? A handmade nail has a rounded top and uneven edges. Some people think they look like roses, thus they are called *rose-headed nails*. Ask an antique dealer to show you one.

Machine-made nails are often referred to as *square nails* since they were made square. These nails were introduced in 1790, but cabinetmakers continued to use handmade nails until about 1840 because

ABOVE: The walls are laden with goodies at this Toronto shop.
FACING PAGE: Offered by the Perkinses, this Neoclassical corner cupboard is from Maryhill in Waterloo County.

they were better nails, being less brittle and breakable and not rusting or deteriorating as easily. As well, since the metal had been worked over by a hammer, it was tighter and therefore stronger. The handmade nail and then the machine-made nail were used in Canada until 1890, when the round wire nail, the nail we know today, appeared.

Machine-cut dovetails are also a quick age gauge. They began appearing in the 1870s. If your furniture has square nails and hand-cut dovetails, then it's more than one hundred years old.

Sheldon believes that the question of restoration differs with each piece. Simply put, a Rolls Royce is worth restoring. He would rather see a cornice replaced and repainted than missing altogether. As a general rule, you should try to buy an antique with most of its primary wood original. (The primary wood is everything that shows. What doesn't show is referred to as secondary wood.)

Some final advice from Sheldon. Only buy from dealers who tag their merchandise, explaining what the piece is and where it's from. After the purchase, keep that tag with the piece for future reference. Sheldon believes that the best way to build a collection is to establish a relationship with two or three reputable dealers, then purchase the best quality you possibly can for the money you have to spend.

R. G. Perkins and Son Antiques:
1198 Yonge Street, Toronto
Open Monday to Friday 10:30 A.M. – 6:00 P.M.,
Saturday 10:30 A.M. – 5:00 P.M.
(416) 925-0973

30

R.A. O'Neil Antiques Ltd.

Proportion—The Key to Quality

"**Q**uality is our standard, not country of origin," says June O'Neil. Back in the late 1960s she and her husband, Bob, began going out on Saturdays, buying antique clocks and guns. They would buy here, sell there and make enough money to go out for supper that night.

Bob had an eye for antiques—an eye that June, like Marjorie Larmon of the Pig 'n' Plow, contends you have to be born with. He had developed and refined that eye by visiting museums everywhere he went as he travelled the world in his late teens. In 1969 Bob made his first picking trip to Nova Scotia. He took $1,000 and a rented trailer. Before he left he was told by another dealer that he was wasting his time because all the good Canadiana was gone. But he filled his truck with so much furniture that he

had to tie it down with a fish net—and he came home with money left over.

For the next twelve years Bob made a trip to Quebec or the Maritimes every week, while June kept the home fires burning. He wholesaled most of what he bought to other dealers. He hated the driving but he loved the pleasure of the great find: an armoire carved with animals and seagrass, a set of six matching bowback Windsor chairs, not one but two diamond-point armoires found in the same barn. In 1981 Bob and June opened R.A. O'Neil Antiques Limited on Avenue Road in Toronto. June contends it was the best move they ever made.

Initially they planned on selling painted furniture only. If they had stuck to that plan, June thinks, they might have starved to death. Today they specialize in nineteenth-century pine country furniture from

Ontario, Quebec, Nova Scotia, the British Isles, Scandinavia, Italy and France.

Furniture of Canadian origin is a mosaic of that from all the European countries. English dish dressers, Scandinavian wardrobes, Irish settle beds, French armoires: all made their way to Canada as memories in the minds of settlers. Skilled craftsmen made their way here too, and they began to build those memories for the burgeoning Canadian furniture market. It's an education to wander around the O'Neils' large shop, comparing European and Canadian styles. Borders blur,

since English pine furniture was made with Canadian white pine. More than fifty percent of the British pieces the O'Neils carry are made with Canadian pine. Our pine was the best-quality pine in the world, and since the wood was in great supply here and short supply overseas, it was exported to the British Isles. It made perfect ballast in the trade ships. It's interesting to note that mahogany made its way from the West Indies to the Maritime provinces in the same way.

Both Bob and June O'Neil feel that proportion is the most important quality to look for in pine—or in any—furniture. "When you're looking at a piece and the proportions are right, it jumps out at you." It's wonderful when something is old. Better still if you think it's a good investment. However, you have to live with your furniture every day, so buy only what you love.

That's the advice of seasoned antique dealers.

ABOVE: The O'Neils look for good form and proportion in the furnishings they sell.
FACING PAGE: Imported and Canadian country furniture mix well in this Avenue Road shop.

R.A. O'Neil Antiques Ltd.:
Bob and June O'Neil
100 Avenue Road, Toronto
Open Monday to Saturday 11:00 A.M. – 5:00 P.M.
(416) 968-2806

Recommended Reading:
Antiques: An Illustrated Guide for the Canadian Collector, Hyla Fox

31

Linda Howard Antiques
Portneuf and Other Mysteries

Back in 1968, when Linda Howard began collecting antiques, there was very little documentation on the subject. She recalls searching through the small publication *In a Canadian Attic*, by Gerald Stevens, trying to find the answers to an abundance of questions. She eventually found most answers simply through trial and error and years of research and experience.

Linda's first shop was in Uxbridge, but in 1986 she moved it to its present location on Mount Pleasant Road in Toronto. Along with the finest of country furniture and accessories, a specialty of her shop is pottery called sponge-ware, spatter-ware, and gaudy-ware.

These earthenware pieces date from the middle to the last quarter of the nineteenth century. They were made in Staffordshire, England, and the Swansea area of south Wales. Cheap and brightly decorated, sponge- and spatter-ware appealed to people in country areas, and vast quantities were shipped to North America. In fact, so much sponge-ware was found in Portneuf County in Quebec that it was believed for many years that it was actually produced somewhere in that area. The term *Portneuf* pottery became synonymous with sponge-ware.

It must be remembered that Britain's view of her colonies was always as a source of raw materials and a ready market. Industry was never encouraged. For this reason, large English porcelain and pottery factories made a great deal of merchandise strictly for export.

The colourful designs on sponge-ware were made with a stamp carved from the tightly grained root end of the sponge plant. This method was simple, and the stamp, much like a carved potato stamp, was easily made. Spatter-ware was decorated by hitting a paint-filled brush with a finger, letting the colours spatter over the plate, bowl, or cup. It is thought that this decoration of sponge- and spatter-ware was often done by children, as this was the Dickensian era of child labour in factories.

Linda Howard's shop also features Canadian historical china. These are pieces decorated with Canadian scenes taken

78

ABOVE: This view from the entrance of Linda Howard Antiques displays many of her country dining furnishings and accessories.
FACING PAGE: This New Brunswick open dish dresser was originally an architectural build-in.

from prints. Some were made as early as the 1820s, but they were most popular in the middle of the nineteenth century. Like sponge- and spatter-ware, this china was made for export to the Canadian market by the large porcelain and pottery factories in Great Britain.

In the world of Canadian antiques everything becomes a wonderful puzzle to be solved. That solution always results in a greater understanding of who we are and where we came from. The best part is this: the Canadian antique search is in its infancy, with many mysteries still to unfold.

Linda Howard Antiques:
Linda Howard
661 Mount Pleasant Road, Toronto
Open Tuesday to Saturday 10:00 A.M. –
6:00 P.M.
(416) 485-2283

Recommended Reading:
Nineteenth Century Pottery and Porcelain of Canada, Elizabeth Collard

Take a few minutes to visit the other antique shops located on Mount Pleasant Road within a few blocks of Linda Howard Antiques.

32

Town of York
Defining Georgian Formal Furniture

Bob Starr of Town of York antique shop never wants to retire. He hopes that when his end comes, he'll be carried out of his shop in the best Georgian storage chest he owns.

You'll find Town of York, not unnaturally, in what was once the town of York. And the shop's proprietor knows Toronto well: since he opened in 1974, Town

of York has hit all the hot spots—Markham Street, the St. Lawrence Market, Yorkville, and Avenue Road. Today the shop makes its home on Davenport Road, on Designer's Row, among galleries of both art and antiques.

Bob's wife, Brenda, is a graduate of the Ontario College of Art, and it was her interest in Canadian art

RIGHT: A Thomas Nisbet (Saint John, N.B., 1780–1851) desk is typical of the quality and period of Town of York's goods.
FACING PAGE: For Canadian and European formal furnishings from the Georgian period, try Town of York.

that first led them to an appreciation of Canada's earliest antiques. When they started in the antique business they were strictly interested in country furniture and folk art. Their tastes have changed with time, and now they deal primarily in formal furniture of the Georgian period from both Britain and Canada.

The Georgian period, so named because it spanned the consecutive reigns of four British kings named George, began in 1714 and ended in 1830, just as steam power began to affect the furniture industry in Europe. Georgian furniture thus marks the end of an era—the era of completely handmade furniture.

The Great Fire of London during the Georgian period was a boon for the English furniture industry: a great deal of English formal furniture dates to the first quarter of the nineteenth century, having been built to replace what had been lost in the fire. It was during this time that the Regency style appeared. Perhaps the most significant feature of Regency furniture is reeding, decorative carving of ribbed, or reed-like, strips.

In Canada, the cities of Montreal and St. John were the main centres of Georgian formal furniture. Upper Canada and the muddy town of York were too young and too sparsely populated at that time to support a large furniture industry.

According to Bob there are a number of things that help us to recognize Georgian formal furniture. First, the piece must closely follow a design, be it Chippendale, Adam, Hepplewhite, Sheraton or Regency. Canadian formal pieces often show transitional elements of these styles; in other words, more than one style might be incorporated in the same piece. Cabinetmakers would never choose pine as the primary wood for a formal piece. The wood was chosen to complement the formal style. In Canada, our indigenous woods—maple (particularly bird's-eye and tiger), cherry and birch—were used. Mahogany was shipped to Canada from the West Indies but went no further west than Montreal, the end of shipping on the St. Lawrence at that time. Remembering that black walnut is a wood that grows only in North America is an easy way to trace the origin of formal walnut pieces. Secondary woods can also provide clues to origin.

Bob enjoys sharing what he has learned about Georgian and Regency furniture with anyone who visits him in his shop. No doubt he will continue to do so until they carry him out of there in a Georgian chest.

Town of York:
Robert and Brenda Starr
184 Davenport Road, Toronto
Tuesday to Sunday 10:30 A.M. – 5:00 P.M.
(416) 925-4720

Recommended Reading:
English Canadian Furniture of the Georgian Period,
Donald Blake Webster

33

Hugh Anson-Cartwright
Antiquarian Books

Hugh Anson-Cartwright was a man full of questions in 1966 when he took the plunge and made his hobby into his livelihood. "I've been learning about books ever since," says Hugh. It took him some time to realize that it was better to buy one great book than several mediocre ones. He then grew to understand the many points of reference from which book collectors pursue this varied pastime.

Interest, importance, beauty, rarity and condition are all considerations. Each collector will place these in a different order.

You'll find the workmanship that went into the manufacture of an old book something of rare beauty. Remember that early books were bound by hand. Leather bindings, explains Hugh, were made from the untanned but degreased inner portion of the split skin of an animal. If that animal was a sheep, such covers are called *parchment*. Calfskin covers are referred to as *vellum*. Often, these covers were decorated with intricate gold stamping.

By the 1850s publishers were using cloth covers. Victorian stamping and colour printing were publishing innovations, as were tipped-in pictures (secured by a narrow line of paste on one side). All are of interest to collectors. Books with marbled edges or marbled endpapers have added merit. If you have in your hand a leather-bound, gold-stamped, marble-edged book, you are holding something that would be very costly to produce today.

Hugh explains that with old books, just as with old china, if there's a chip, the price goes down. "Chips" on a book might be such things as *foxing* (a fungus that attacks paper, turning it brown), water stains, broken back strips, and torn or missing pages.

The most sought-after early Canadian books are those of travel and exploration; for example, *Mackenzie's Voyages* (first edition, London, 1801) or *Sir J. Ross's Second Voyage, 1835*. Modern first editions by prominent writers such as Robertson Davies or Margaret Laurence are very collectable.

As you can imagine, lovers of books produce books about books, so the subject is very well documented. Many antiquarian book dealers also sell old maps, prints, and photographs.

Questions about the past? You might find the answers in an antiquarian book.

ABOVE: You can easily lose yourself in the world of antiquarian books.
FACING PAGE: A shelf of ancient words at Hugh Anson-Cartwright.

Hugh Anson-Cartwright:
 229 College Street, Toronto
Open Tuesday to Friday 9:30 A.M. – 5:30 P.M.,
Saturday 10:00 A.M. – 5:00 P.M.
(416) 979-2441

For other antiquarian book dealers see *Bookguide: Antiquarian Book, Map, Print Dealers of Ontario*, published by Highway Bookshop, Cobalt, Ontario, or *Toronto and Area Directory of Antiquarian Booksellers*, available at most antiquarian bookshops in Toronto.

Visit:
The Osborne Collection of Early Children's Books at Toronto Public Library;
The Market Gallery at St. Lawrence Market, 2nd Floor, to see rotating displays from the Toronto Archives;

Antiquarian Bookfairs in Toronto and Ottawa.
Phone David Mason (416) 598-1015 for more information.

Recommended Reading:
ABC for Book Collectors, John Carter
A Dictionary of Toronto Printers, Publishers, Booksellers and the Allied Trades, 1798–1900
Collected Books—The Guide to Values, Allen and Patricia Ahearn

34

Sarah Gresham Antiques
Adorning Yourself in History

Hand-done beadwork, handmade lace, hand-woven trim, handsewn sequins: all the little details, the mystical lingering presence in each careful stitch.

Marjorie Maloney has operated Sarah Gresham Antiques (named for her daughter) on Queen Street in Toronto since 1985, catering to the clothing collector's desire to adorn oneself with history. For Marjorie, it is first the overall cut or design of a vintage garment and then that attention to detail that is her measure of quality.

Her attention to particulars was developed while she attended art college. Initially, she collected clothing, jewellery, fountain pens, and linens. "I was always interested in well-crafted things," she explains. While she was growing up, her mother sewed and did needlework, so she was well versed in the technical aspects of handwork.

Asked how old clothing must be before it is considered "vintage," Marjorie replies that, for her, clothing from the 1940s would be of little interest. Her personal favourites are "flapper" outfits from the Roaring Twenties and lovely lacey Victorian underwear with every seam handstitched with love.

Since fabric does deteriorate with age, clothing is a fugitive collection, Marjorie explains. Her customers buy vintage clothes to wear them. Clothing from the twenties is very popular for evening wear. Finely detailed lawn (a very fine cotton) christening gowns are bought for baby's special day. Helping a bride to find something old and something blue is an interesting part of her business.

Handmade lace, whether lace collars or adornments on clothing, linens or tablecloths, is always sought after. Marjorie always uses a magnifying glass to examine old lace, to tell whether it is handmade or machine-made lace. With practise you too can learn to identify the hand-done version.

Once you've found that special garment, the search for just the right accessories begins. Beaded bags are reminiscent of the era when women still kept dance cards. Chatelaines, carriers which were clipped onto the belt to hold such important things as a pair of scissors, a small perfume bottle, a pencil, or an ivory writing pad, are from an era with strict social rules—an era long gone but magically recalled when you put on its trappings: kid gloves, antique jewellery, satin and lace. The sudden realization that in clothing, nothing is new, as you find a Victorian garment made with glittering metallic thread—fantasy abounds when you play dress-up with clothes from another era.

Sarah Gresham Antiques:
Marjorie Maloney
217 Queen Street East, Toronto
Open Monday to Saturday 12:00 P.M. – 6:00 P.M.
(416) 865-1758

Recommended Reading:
Identification and Value Guide for Old Lace and Linens, Maryanne Dolan
Lace—The Elegant Web, Janine Montapet and Ghislaine Schoeller

While in this vicinity of Queen Street visit the other antique shops.
Visit the Vintage Clothing Sale at the Chateau Laurier in Ottawa, the Old Clothing Show in Toronto in September, or the Toronto Vintage Clothing and Textile Show in March and November. Contact June Troy (905) 666-0523 or (905) 666-3277.

ABOVE: Linens and laces evoke memories of bygone times.
BELOW LEFT: Jewellery and accessories pre-1940.
BELOW RIGHT: Vintage clothes are a favourite with the owner of this Queen Street shop.

35

The Stiver House Gifts Ltd.

An Historic House and Refinished Pine

The Newnham family got into the antique business by accident.

When Mrs. Newnham inherited the historically significant Stiver House in Unionville, the family wasn't sure just what to do with it. One of only two adobe-brick houses surviving in Ontario, the house had been built in 1829 by the first group of Lutheran settlers brought to the area from Pennsylvania by William Berczy. Berczy had been fortunate to find a doctor, Dr. Eckardt, who agreed to accompany the settlers—on condition they would build him a house to live in. When the newcomers dug the hole for the doctor's house, they found clay. They added straw and led a team of oxen around in the excavation to press the clay and straw together. From this mixture they made the adobe brick for the Stiver House.

Mrs. Newnham's great-grandfather, a Stiver, purchased the house in 1874, and it has been in the family ever since.

In 1980 the family decided to open a gift shop in the historic house. Bill and Marein had furnished their own home with pine, and they brought some of their pieces to the store to display merchandise. Customers kept asking if they could buy the antique furniture. After five years of saying it wasn't for sale, Bill and Marein's sons, Thom and Don, decided that maybe refinished pine furniture was what they should be selling. It was definitely in demand.

The Newnhams buy things that need very few repairs, and strip and refinish them inside and out, just as they did with the furniture in their own home. They even refinish the backs of pieces, something that is very popular with their customers, since people often use cupboards as room dividers.

Built in 1829, this rare adobe-brick building is the home of The Stiver House Gifts Ltd., a business that's a family affair.

Sometimes the overpaint is so thick on a piece of pine when they buy it that the features don't show. Once they uncovered a drawer that had been painted shut and then painted over so many times that you couldn't even tell it was there! They were hoping the drawer would be filled with jewels, but no such luck.

"We aren't selling museum pieces," says Thom, "but one thing you must remember is that every antique is unique." He hates to see customers disappointed by deliberating too long over a piece. "When purchasing antiques, and this is true for dealers as well as clients, the unfortunate truth is, if you snooze, you lose," he muses. When that piece is gone, you can't ever get another exactly the same.

Though they began in the antique business by chance, the business has been very good to them. Their large inventory of Canadian pine from the late 1700s to the late 1800s is still used to display

The Stiver House Gifts is an antique shop and a gift store, and these Mennonite cupboards from Waterloo County, circa 1860, function as their display shelves for new gift items.

new gift items. At The Stiver House you might be greeted by Marein, Bill, Thom, Don, or their sister Susan, all Newnhams involved in this family business that began because of a historic adobe-brick house in Unionville.

The Stiver House Gifts Ltd.:
The Newnhams
206 Main Street, Unionville
Open Monday to Saturday 11:00 A.M. – 5:00 P.M.,
Sunday 12:00 P.M. – 5:00 P.M.
Closed Mondays in the winter months
(905) 477-1585, (905) 223-6769

Unionville is a day-trip town where you can spend some time touring.

36

Michael Rowan Antiques
Prairie Folk Furniture

When Henry Ford said, "I am collecting the history of our people as written into things their hands made and used," he was providing a definition of folk art. Folk art, the art of the common people, has interested Michael Rowan since he opened his business in 1971. You might discover other things in this shop too—anything from eighteenth-century formal furniture to Art Deco pieces, but Michael's business card reads "Traditional Folk Art," and although no sign hangs outside his home in Green River, enthusiasts of folk art, particularly folk furniture, find Michael anyway.

In the early years, when Michael visited museums, he learned that Quebec folk art dominated the field, so he decided to concentrate on folk art that didn't come from that province. He was looking for Wilno

furniture (Polish traditional folk furniture from an area northwest of Ottawa), when a friend introduced him to folk furniture from the western provinces. It excited him and he began to seek out furniture, textiles and other domestic items made by the waves of Ukrainian, Doukhobor, Hutterite and Mennonite settlers who had arrived in the harsh environment of the newly opened Canadian West in the years surrounding the turn of the century. Currently Michael is hard at work on a book about prairie folk furniture, following on the heels of a catalogue he and John Fleming put together about Ukrainian furniture.

Prairie folk art shows the specific cultural traditions of those ethnic communities—mainly eastern European—which settled the prairies. They had all arrived in the west following long journeys. The Hutterites, for example, a communal pacifist sect formed in 1528, had moved from western Europe to the Ukraine, then to South Dakota, and finally, in 1918, to the Canadian prairies. The Ukrainians originated in the Ukraine, the Doukhobors in Russia, the Mennonites and Hutterites had German roots. All were in search of a homeland where they could preserve those cultural and spiritual differences which they had tenaciously held onto for several centuries, in spite of the constant threat from modern ideas and ideologies.

Michael describes prairie folk furniture as predictable. The styles are old, remembered styles. Made of pine and spruce and fir, the furniture is painted in bright yellows, reds and greens, often highlighted with black. Frequently it is decorated with flowers, birds and other folk motifs such as hearts, fans and pin-

LEFT: Arrowback chairs made by Gibbard from Napanee, Ontario (1840–1850), complement a Ukrainian painted table made in Yorkton, Saskatchewan, sixty years later.
FACING PAGE: Doukhobor, Ukrainian, Hutterite, and Mennonite furniture and accessories from Western Canada, ethnic folk art at its best.

wheels—symbols of long-held beliefs and superstitions. Every colour is rich with ancient symbolic meaning. The furniture makes a strong statement of an isolated people little known or understood by the rest of Canada.

Though folk art is often described as the art of the untrained, this particular folk art called for training, explains Michael. For instance, in the Hutterite community, extensive embroidering and cross-stitching were commonly done on factory-made linens. These textile pieces required skills—skills taught and mastered, then shown off in a brilliant and colourful profusion of motifs.

Think for a moment what was happening in other parts of North America as Hutterite girls quietly stitched these tokens of love. They practised their handiwork for hours on samplers and towels while North American cities were in the grip of the Roaring Twenties. A liberated generation of flappers was celebrating life in grand style: riding on the tops of taxis, sipping champagne out of slippers, and jumping, clothes and all, into foaming fountains.

Western life was a struggle for every settler. Against a bleak and sometimes harsh prairie, those ethnic communities expressed their need for colour, form and continuity through the things they made with their hands and used in their daily lives. It is the decorative aspect of those pieces that draws collectors today: the brightness of their colours, the flamboyance and hope of those symbols of age-old customs, their pinwheels, hearts and fans. Perhaps people find in those long-preserved traditions a way of understanding their own hopes and dreams.

Michael Rowan Antiques:
Michael Rowan
Green River, southwest corner of Highway 7 and
Sideroad 34
(905) 471-5511

Ukrainian Furniture by Michael Rowan and John Fleming is available from the Ukrainian Museum at Saint Vladimir Ukrainian Institute, 620 Spadina Avenue, Toronto, Ontario, M5S 2H4. (416) 923-3318

37

Pollikers
Mennonite and Maritime Furniture

*P*olliker is an Irish term for an antique picker. Gerry Marks (nicknamed Swampy), a Canadian picker-dealer for many years, named his Greenwood shop Pollikers.

Gerry's many contacts in Ontario Mennonite communities and in the Maritimes have been the backbone of his business. He is attracted to these places, he thinks, because his pursuit of antiquity probably stems from an interest in a simpler way of life, a way of life found in both these communities. The Mennonite lifestyle, says Gerry, is based on "good families, good neighbours, close communities." Mennonite furniture reflects the beliefs of the people. Styles were repeated over and over because this culture encouraged communal existence, not individuality, creativity and competitiveness. If a style of cupboard worked, then it was used again and again. By the same token, quality of construction was emphasized because things were made to be functional and to last. Nineteenth-century Maritime country furniture is often eccentric, made with primitive construction techniques which denote a lack not only of training, but of materials, of time, and of funds. These pieces reflect the geographic isolation of the Maritimers.

One day Gerry met a man who built new Mennonite furniture and delivered it by horse and buggy. Why, he enquired, would the man not buy a truck? It would make deliveries so much easier for him. "If I had a truck," the man replied, "I'd be tempted to drive to Niagara Falls and then I'd spend money I didn't have. Better to stick with my horse and buggy."

Similarly, he remembers a Maritimer trying to explain why his modest, often difficult existence, on a small property with a few sheep meant so much to him. "If a man loses his land," the farmer said simply, "he loses everything."

To Gerry, these two stories say all that needs to be said about the lifestyle and beliefs he admires.

Like so many of the dealers in this book, Gerry's advice when asked what to look for when purchasing antique Mennonite furniture or pieces from the Maritimes is simple: buy what you like and what you can identify with. Buy what speaks to you.

No doubt both the Maritimers and the Mennonites, with their straightforward approaches to life, would agree.

LEFT AND FACING PAGE: For pine aplenty with a special interest in the Maritimes and Mennonite furniture, visit Pollikers.

Pollikers:
Gerry Marks
Greenwood
(905) 427-4498

Across the street, visit the Pickering Township
Pioneer Village.

38

The Brooklin Antiquarian
On the Road Again

Dave Stewart is a man who spends a great deal of time on the road. He sets up at fifteen to twenty antique shows a year—an impressive record even for show people. Because of this, he warns, his shop, The Brooklin Antiquarian, is in a constant state of flux—if he's not barely home from a show when you visit, he might just be leaving.

But don't let this dissuade you from stopping in. Dave carries an impressive display of refinished Canadian country furniture. He looks for the unusual, unique or slightly off-beat in a piece—a table with a top made of only one board, a cupboard with adjustable shelving, a chest of drawers with a hidden compartment. "I set my own standards and I stick to them," Dave explains. Those standards include selling good-quality pieces with few repairs and absolutely no alterations.

Alteration in the antique business differs a great deal from restoration. Making a sideboard into a dry sink is *alteration*. Putting a new top on a set of table legs is *alteration*. Changing a piece in any way from its original form is *alteration*. Once an alteration is done, the piece loses its antique value and becomes merely furniture.

Like most antique dealers, Dave started as a collector. He dabbled in the auction business, and then, in 1975, he established The Brooklin Antiquarian in Brooklin, north of Whitby.

Dave's advice for a novice collector is to attend a quality antique show—you'll get your feet very, very wet in short order. If it's an outdoor show, just hope that it doesn't rain or you can take that literally. When you make the decision to buy antiques, always buy the best possible quality you can afford. Be patient, suggests Dave; buy only one or two good pieces a year and build up your collection slowly as you learn.

ABOVE: These matching display cupboards with many drawers are an example of the slightly off-beat furniture that Dave Stewart enjoys selling.
FACING PAGE: Dave looks for the unusual in a piece, like these glazed cupboards, one with a bank of drawers below, and the other with multi-panes and no step-back.

The Brooklin Antiquarian:
Dave Stewart
Brooklin
(905) 655-3723

Some of Dave's favourite shows:
The Elora Antique Show and Sale in Elora in the fall;
In Toronto—Waltzing Through Time at the O'Keefe Centre;
The Toronto Antique Show and Sale (sponsored by Wimodausis);
In Ottawa—The Ashbury College Antique Fair;
The Capital Antique Show;

The Muskoka Antique Show in Port Carling mid-summer;
Antiques at Trafalgar Castle in Whitby;
Outdoors—The Christie Classic spring and fall.

If you can only afford two books buy:
The Heritage of Upper Canadian Furniture, Howard Pain
The Early Furniture of French Canada, Jean Palardy

39

Patricia Price
'Twas Ever Thus

Patricia Price welcomes collectors, both seasoned and novice, to her shop just outside Manchester, a hamlet near Port Perry. Patricia understands collectors well. Since the 1960s she and her husband, Ralph, have been almost insatiable collectors themselves.

When the Prices began their collection, searching for unique decorative antique items which they thought would complement their early Canadian painted furniture, they found themselves selecting vernacular pieces made of wood, metal, and fabric which spoke of individual thoughts and ideas. The pieces they chose told of early Canada and the personal spirit of its people. Though they didn't understand it at the beginning, they were among the first few looking for examples of Canadian folk art.

The definitive definition of Canadian folk art has been discussed at length and just about everything you read on the subject will contain contradictions. Canada is young, large, and lacks homogeneity. We couldn't possibly have developed any one distinct tradition among our ordinary folk. Yet, individuals will create. They will whittle and pare, sew distinctive quilts, hook unique rugs, and design their own metal weather vanes.

These items become folk art, Patricia believes, when that carved-wood ornament or that naïve painting has a heart, a heart that you can almost feel beating, the heart of its maker. This individual had a unique vision and the ability to express that vision without any formal training. If you feel something when you look at that creation, then it's folk art.

Using this as their guide, by 1978 the Prices had put together a folk-art collection impressive enough to warrant a show at the Robert McLaughlin Gallery in Oshawa, Ontario. They called the show "'Twas Ever Thus." In the preface of the show's catalogue, gallery director Joan Murray had this to say about the reasons for the show: "Folk art is so vigorous and dynamic that it is hard to define. In general its essence is spontaneity; the work may also be considered naïve, primitive or regional…in Port Perry, in the region of Durham, there is a collection—a major one in Canada—of this material."

The Prices' shop grew out of this collection. In it you'll find

BELOW: Canadian folk pieces enrich Canadian country furnishings at Patricia Price's shop in Manchester. FACING PAGE: Fashioned for a loved child, this late 19th-century toy riding horse from Quebec explains the nature of folk art better than any words could.

painted country furniture in original finishes, along with folk art—particularly weather vanes, quilts, rugs, decoys and carvings. They also offer contemporary folk art. Most of their wares are from Ontario, Quebec and the Maritimes.

In the early days of this country the fight for survival was the primary struggle—so much to do, so little time. Still, somehow, those early settlers managed to break through their workaday world and create something beautiful and lasting, something funny, something that touches us today.

Patricia Price:
Patricia and Ralph Price
Manchester, from Highways 7 and 12, turn right on 7A, then right again at Rose Street
A call ahead is advisable (905) 985-7644

Suggested visits:
Fennimore House, Cooperstown, New York

Recommended Reading:
From the Heart: Folk Art in Canada published in co-operation with the Canadian Centre for Folk Culture Studies, National Museum of Civilization, and National Museums of Canada
Folk Art, Primitive and Naïve Art in Canada, Blake McKendry
Twentieth Century American Folk Art and Artists, Hemphill & Weissman
'Twas Ever Thus, the catalogue for the show at the McLaughlin Gallery

40

J.W. Humphries Antiques Ltd.
Period Collecting

John Humphries wants people to have fun as they browse through antique shops. John has been in the antique business since 1973, and he has always been interested in social history and the development of Canada—serious subjects. But material history, says John, the things that people surrounded themselves with during any given historical period, makes understanding social history not just fascinating but fun.

Take the late Georgian period, called by some "The Golden Age of Furniture," a period when outside influences first showed on the home furnishings of English Lower Canada, the Maritime provinces, and to a lesser extent, Upper Canada. This was a time when Great Britain produced the major designers—Chippendale, Hepplewhite, Sheraton, and Adam—designers who emphasized simplicity of design and published pattern books of their furniture designs. These books made their way around the world, widely influencing the public's taste. The craft tradition still reigned during the Georgian period.

Now, just for fun, take a much later period in Canada, say the 1950s. What was it like in the homes of the 1950s? This was the beginning of the television era. Living rooms were designed around this highly desirable piece of furniture and included such items as

RIGHT: Blue willow, flow blue, cut glass, and many other pleasant surprises await you at this shop in Lindsay. FACING PAGE: A few of John's favourite things.

portable TV tables from which to consume TV dinners. Pottery was popular—a long, sleek black panther might adorn the television set, or perhaps a pair of red Oriental ladies. Lamps with bases of lime green, grey or maroon lit the room.

The other aspect of 1950s furniture, as well as much else of the era, was size. Everything was hugely rounded; cars had large fins sticking out behind. "The bigger the better" was the motto of the fifties. Quality was measured in weight and size—big cars, big radios, big televisions, big everything.

If you were to design for yourself a 1950s room, a sort of private *Happy Days* set that you could live in for a while, wouldn't you begin to understand the people of that time better?

John Humphries feels that in the same way you can admire and understand the late Georgian period or the Regency period, life in an early settlement

cabin, the Victorian era, or the 1920s. The things that people made and used give us a better appreciation of them and of their life. Perhaps furniture of the Georgian period is beyond your means, but that doesn't mean you are unable to collect Canada's material past. If you can't afford Georgian, then pick a period you can afford. Leave your mind open and, above all, have fun.

J.W. Humphries Antiques Ltd.:
John Humphries
9 Russell Street East, Lindsay
Open Tuesday to Saturday 10:00 A.M. – 5:00 P.M.,
Sunday 1:00 P.M. – 5:00 P.M.
Call for winter hours
(705) 324-5050

EASTERN ONTARIO

Canadian country furnishings inside the barn at Blanch Lynn's north of Westbrook.

41

C. Benson Antiques and Smith's Creek Antiques
Ignoring Market Trends

Clay Benson has experienced many changes in the antique market over the years. "The antique market is resilient," says Clay, "but you must remember that it is not immune to outside economic influences."

C. Benson Antiques is the name Clay and Carol Benson gave their first business. Clay still operates this business today. His interest is in eighteenth-, nineteenth-, and early twentieth-century furnishings and art objects in their original condition.

Clay and Carol were so young when they opened that first antique shop twenty-five years ago that they were known around the business as "the kids." Clay had started selling antiques when he was seventeen. He was "the kid" of Madeleine Benson, who's bought and sold antiques for as long as Clay can remember, and Clay grew up attending auctions. Today Carol and Madeleine Benson and two other partners, Elizabeth Rose and David Simmons, operate another shop in downtown Port Hope, called Smith's Creek Antiques. Here you'll find a large selection of refin-

ished country and formal furnishings, plus pottery, porcelains, glassware and lighting.

In his lifetime spent watching the business, Clay has observed many market trends. Brass beds, for example: in twenty-five years, brass beds have enjoyed four surges of popularity in the marketplace. Such mass popularity inflates the price, perhaps unrealistically, but explains Clay's contention that antiques possess two values. The first is market value, what a given market will pay in dollars at a given time. The second is real value. Real value is based on the quality of the item relative to others in the same category. As a buyer, you should understand and respect the reasons behind both prices.

If you rely on your own personal taste and not mass taste, then you are less apt to be swayed by market trends and more apt to base your purchasing on real value. Determine, first of all, your reasons for purchasing an antique. Are you buying it as an investment? Are you buying it as a functional item? Or are you buying it simply for the personal satisfaction of owning it?

Collecting antiques is a learning process for everyone, and therein lies the true pleasure. You can read about those things that interest you, but you must also get out and experience them in other ways. Ownership is the best teacher. When you're looking at antique items and trying to develop your own personal taste, look for things that strike you as being more than the sum of their parts. Talk to other collectors and to dealers about your interest. Try to connect with the history of the item you are viewing—where it came from, its original function, and its place in the fabric of your heritage. Finally, and perhaps most importantly, connect with it from the heart.

That's what Clay and Carol started doing back when they were called "the kids." That's what still motivates C. Benson Antiques and Smith's Creek Antiques today.

ABOVE: A secretary in tiger maple from Western Ontario, circa 1860.
FACING PAGE: An 1890s English exotic bird study and a mahogany roll-top desk, circa 1880, are among the rarities to be found at this shop.

C. Benson Antiques:
Clay Benson
Port Hope
Please call for an appointment
(905) 885-8000

Smith's Creek Antiques:
M. Benson, C. Benson, E. Rose, and D. Simmons
27 Walton Street, Port Hope
Open daily
(905) 885-7840

Recommended reading:
At Home in Upper Canada, Jeanne Minhinnick

Bluestone House in Port Hope publishes "Canada's magazine for today's traditional home." For more information write to *Century Home*, 12 Mill Street South, Port Hope, Ontario, L1A 2S5.

42

Van Schyndel–Lachapelle Antiques
Celebrating the Armoire

In Quebec they say that if an English person has a thousand dollars he or she will put down a new floor in the kitchen; a French person will take a thousand dollars and throw a party. This facet of the French personality translates itself to the early furniture of the province. French-Canadian antiques embody an element of artistic flair which is a pleasure to behold. Early French-Canadian craftsmen were never afraid to add a few frills. They built furniture which was practical and useful, but which at the same time was a celebration.

This flamboyance of design is hard to resist, and after twenty-five years in the business, Lynn Van Schyndel and Gabriel Lachapelle have succumbed to it completely. They specialize in furniture and folk art of early French Canada in its original paint. Van Schyndel–Lachapelle Antiques of Grafton display their French-Canadian treasures in a log cabin built by Gabriel.

Asked to outline her requirements for a quality armoire (the French word for a cupboard)—an

Two Quebec armoires—can you pick out their distinguishing features?

armoire worth celebrating—Lynn gives originality and condition as her primary considerations. The most exciting pieces for her are those that have not been altered in any way. When there is no restoration needed and the piece retains not only its original paint but also its original hardware, that's quality!

Age is the second factor of importance. The very best Quebec pieces date to the seventeenth century, because Lower Canada, unlike Upper Canada, was quite extensively settled at that time.

After originality and age comes the detail of the piece. The doors of the armoire are built in frames which hold raised panels (panels which extend outwards beyond the frame). Made from a thicker board, these are bevelled or chamfered (cut on a slant to reduce the thickness) into the frame. Double raised panels (panels which are raised twice) indicate an older piece. Better armoires have raised panels on the ends or sides as well as on the doors. The more raised panels that an armoire sports, the better it is considered to be.

It is important that a good armoire retains its original hand-forged hardware. The doors of earlier cupboards were overlapping; they sat out from the cupboard frame and overlapped it all the way around. This required a different type of hinge, called a *fische hinge*, which allowed the doors to lift completely off the frames. A fische hinge was made in two parts: a pin or pivot post attached to the frame and a wrought-iron cylinder attached to the door to slip over this pin. Pic and barrel hinges are exactly as described and very plain. Rat-tail hinges have a decorative tail on the pin part, securing it to the frame. Other types of finishing details called vases, pearls, or balusters sometimes decorate the ends of both pieces of a fische hinge.

The second piece of original hardware to look for is the keyhole escutcheon. Armoires were always made

Quebec lozenge armoire, circa 1680–1700, in pristine untouched condition, with rare pearl fische hinges of the French Regime period.

with a lock and key on one door. On the earlier cupboards this key hole on the door was decorated with a metal escutcheon (surround) cut out of iron in a stylized dragon, sea-horse or flame design.

Having examined the hardware, move to the paint. Make sure the paint is original. Paint that has never been overpainted is Lynn's first choice. Her second choice is a piece stripped to the original colour, a talent possessed by few antique refinishers.

Amidst the revelry there is a warning. Reproducing antiques has become a sophisticated business in Quebec. And even with genuine pieces you must be very cautious. Repaints can be well disguised, and always check doors, cornices and mouldings to see if they have been replaced. Lynn suggests that you have the dealer write all restorations on the bill of purchase for you.

Thinking about a celebration? Why not look for a quality French-Canadian armoire?

Van Schyndel–Lachapelle Antiques:
Lynn Van Schyndel and Gabriel Lachapelle
Grafton
A call ahead is recommended
(905) 349-2467

While in the area, visit:
Larry Foster and Son Antiques at their 1820 Burnham–Foster home.
(905) 372-7255

43

Pine and Time Antiques
"As Found" Antiques

On the shores of the Bay of Quinte south of Napanee, Jon Silver's combined home and place of business overlook a finger of the bay, called Long Reach. On the opposite bank is Prince Edward County, where Jon's ancestors were among the first Loyalists to land and make Canada their home.

Jon is interested in preservation—preservation of pine, preservation of time. His interest takes him out knocking on doors, seeking out antiques. Pine and Time started sixteen years ago. Jon was a teacher at a private school at the time, and he was looking for a way to finance the very good antique pieces he wanted to purchase for himself. In the last few years Pine and Time has become his full-time occupation.

"You never know what you're going to find," Jon says, talking about the unpredictability of door-knocking. This makes his stock eclectic, with, he hopes, something for every taste and pocketbook. He sells everything in "as found" condition. His wares fall into many different categories, and the quality ranges from the common to the very good. There is no question, says Jon, that the availability of very good articles is diminishing.

Jon finds that the public often gets erroneous ideas about the price of antiques. A pine table might sell at auction for a certain price, and people will assume that their table is worth the same. It may be, but it could also be worth twice as much or one-quarter of that price, depending not only on the features of the table, but on its age, its rarity, its condition, and its desirability in the marketplace. Only educating yourself to these differences can make you knowledgeable both as a buyer and a seller. Jon encourages people to read reference books to understand history, styles and details.

There is one other way that Jon shelters time. He is creating a wetland wildlife preserve around existing and new ponds on his sixty-five acres. The preserve will be designed for people to enjoy as well as to learn from. Customers of Pine and Time are invited to bring a picnic and have a swim in the bay, and those with recreational vehicles are welcome to spend the night.

Conservation and preservation go hand in hand at Pine and Time. Jon Silver wants to save not only the past in all its wonder, but also the present, with its natural beauty, for future generations to understand and experience.

Fan-back Windsor chairs marked with the brand stamp T. Wilson, *and a corner cupboard with diamond-point drawer panels from Aylmer (Western Ontario), circa 1840.*

Early Canadian trivets, wall boxes, and whirligigs join other great smalls at Pine and Time Antiques.

Pine and Time Antiques:
A. Jon Silver
Go south of Napanee on Highway 41 to County
Road 9 (River Road). Turn right and go 16.7 km.
Open most times but a call the previous evening is
advisable
(613) 354-3455

Recommended Reading:

For textiles, *To Keep Me Warm One Night*, Dorothy
K. and Harold B. Burnham

For chairs, *The Windsor Style in America*, Volumes I
and II, Charles Santore

44

Blanche Lynn

Provenance—When Seeing Is Believing

In the world of antiques, establishing the provenance of a piece is very important. It can also be very difficult. Blanche Lynn and her husband, Dr. Beverley Lynn, know this from long experience, having spent over thirty years in the antique business.

In antiquer's jargon, *provenance* means the source and possibly the history of something. The maker, the original owner, and the place and time it was made are all important in establishing provenance.

A close-up of the branded stamp showing the chair's maker.

Full provenance is constituted by the maker's signature on a piece. The Lynns have a private collection of signed chairs, with the earliest dating to 1785. Beverley favours chairs signed with either an ink or a branded stamp. Usually the stamp contains the maker's name and place of business. If you know the name of the chairmaker you can do further research. The archives of an area or even its chamber of commerce will provide you with information about the dates of operation of that cabinetmaker.

Beverley quotes a British antiques author who said that *circa*, the Latin for "about" and used in connection with dates, could mean fifty years either side of the given date. He laughs, but points out that there is a serious side to this statement. Chairmakers often operated over a considerable time, thirty to fifty years or even longer. The Hatches, father and son, were chairmakers in Kingston from 1810 to sometime after 1860. Charles Hatch, the father, used a burned stamp to mark his chairs. Wilson, the son, used an ink stamp. This indicates that branded stamps mark earlier

From left to right: Gunstock side chair signed Walters, Bowmanville, *continuous arm Windsor chair stamped* Gammon, *John Newson Boston rocker,* Humeston *Windsor side chair (stamped), nursing rocker made by* Chester Hatch.

chairs. A Hatch chair given the provenance "*c.* 1825" could mean it was built at any time during the Hatches' long career.

Other than chairs by the Hatches, the Lynns count in their collection chairs by the Halifax chairmakers Gammon and Humeston, who always marked their chairs with the word *warranteed*, and an ink-stamped Nova Scotia Sibley chair. Another chair was made by a New Brunswick maker named Hay who died young in 1840. One of the chairs in the Lynn collection has a double provenance. It is stamped with a Canadian chairmaker's name as well as that of G. Robinson of Rochester, New York. No other proof is needed that chair parts crossed the border regularly. This chair must have been shipped from the United States and assembled in Canada.

Sometimes you can establish some provenance through the knowledge of the family from whom the article was purchased. Such word-of-mouth information is certainly better that none, but it must always be remembered that family stories contain a measure of folklore. Old family photographs which show the piece provide a more reliable source of provenance, but they are a very rare find.

The term *attributed to* is often used when describing an antique, and methods of construction can certainly provide clues to the maker, but you should keep in mind that an "attribution" and full provenance are two different things.

The Lynns sell Ontario, Quebec and Maritime furniture from their large barn, where seeing is believing.

Blanche Lynn:
Blanche and Beverley Lynn
North of Westbrook to Concession 4
Please phone for directions
(613) 389-1554

45

Country Lane Antiques

Water Goblets and Chicken Feathers

Bruce Guthrie's interest in antiques began with the purchase of a Model T Ford when he was in grade twelve. Two years later he sold it and bought a Model A. It seemed natural when he needed house furnishings to look for antiques. Thus began a twenty-year hobby that culminated seven years ago when Bruce gave up his office job and turned his hobby into a business, Country Lane Antiques.

"I like to work with my hands," explains Bruce, and the careful restoration and refinishing of nineteenth-century Canadian country furniture allows him to satisfy that need. He strives to preserve the authenticity and the character of each piece he works on. Bruce

A selection of North American flint and pressed glass goblets.

watches for unusual treenware, decoys and pottery to complement his furniture. Water goblets are another favourite, and the shop always stocks them. Today people use them for wine glasses. Even earlier than pressed-glass goblets were flint goblets. They were made between 1840 and 1860. You can tell if a glass is leaded, and thus flint glass, by patterns, which are simpler in flint goblets, and by the sound: when you gently tap a flint goblet, it has a lovely ring to it.

Pressed glass was invented in the United States. By 1876 more than half of the pressed-glass factories in the United States—sixty of them—were located in Pittsburgh. These factories produced glass in literally thousands of patterns.

There is some controversy over how much pressed glass was made in Canada, explains Bruce, even among the experts. Certain Nova Scotia patterns are definably Canadian, but because there is some question about the origin of Canadian glass, to be on the safe side, Bruce prefers to sell his pressed-glass wares as "North American." He suggests that you buy what you like in a goblet without worrying too much about whether it is Canadian or American.

Country Lane Antiques, on the Tay River just outside Glen Tay, offers you the opportunity to pick a piece of furniture in pine,

Flint and pressed-glass goblets and Bruce's carefully restored country furniture are found in the shop at the end of the lane.

butternut or basswood "in the rough" (that is, complete with overpaint, whitewash and chicken feathers) and then have Bruce refinish it for you. This way, explains Bruce, the customer knows exactly what has to be done in the way of repairs.

Country Lane Antiques:
Bruce Guthrie
R.R. 3, Perth (Glen Tay)
Best to call ahead for directions
(613) 267-4686

Recommended reading on water goblets:
American and Canadian Goblets, Doris and Peter Unitt
Early American Pattern Glass, volumes I and II, Alice Hulett Metz
The Collector's Encyclopedia of Pattern Glass, Mollie Helen McCain

In Ottawa, visit 1185 Bank Street. Along with Country Lane Antiques this group shop has a selection of such well-known Ottawa-area dealers as Warren Snider, Locke and Mackenzie, Ashton, Catherine Kerr, Lionel Aubrey, and the Ruhlands.

For more shops in Eastern Ontario, *Antiquing in Eastern Ontario* is published yearly, and the guide map of Perth and area antique shops, available in Perth, is helpful.

46

Greenburnie Antiques Ltd.

Georgian Furniture—A Radical Viewpoint

When Paul Byington quit his teaching job in 1967, he opened Greenburnie Antiques, thinking he would deal in antiques until he could find something more satisfactory to do. Antiques were an obvious choice, since Paul had grown up in the business. His parents, Lovina and Clarence Byington, began selling Victorian furniture in the mid-1950s. Very soon they were encouraged by author, dealer and Canadiana pioneer Gerald Stevens to take the then-extreme step of buying and selling Canadian country furniture.

Paul specializes in pre-1860 country and formal furniture in the Georgian tradition, and in compatible accessories. The Georgian style lingered in this country into the 1860s, thirty years past the reigns of the four King Georges. While formal Canadian furniture was made of walnut, rosewood and mahogany, Georgian country pieces, with very little veneering or inlay work, were only made with indigenous woods, not imported woods. The terms *upper country* and *high country* are used to describe these pieces. In fact, they are in a class that falls between formal furniture and country furniture, and you'll find they will complement either style in a room.

Paul has what he believes might be considered a radical viewpoint on formal Georgian furniture. For years, collectors have understood the importance of retaining original finishes on country furniture, while at the same time, formal furniture has been stripped and French polished until the finish was so perfectly high gloss that you could see your reflection in it. In Georgian times, formal furniture rarely had such a

110

ABOVE: Canadian formal furnishings are a specialty of this shop in the country.
FACING PAGE: Accessories complement formal furnishings at Greenburnie Antiques.

finish. Perhaps the top-of-the-line pieces were French polished, but most pieces were varnished or shellacked, and the look was much softer. Paul believes in only a gentle cleaning for formal pieces, thereby retaining their signs of age and wear. These pieces are over one hundred and fifty years old and they should show that, he insists. Americans are beginning to pay premium prices for untouched formal pieces, and Paul predicts that the trend will move to Canada.

To Paul, this business is a constant learning process. What about that more satisfactory occupation? "I'm still looking," he says.

Greenburnie Antiques Ltd.:
Paul C. Byington
On County Road 1, east of Rideau Ferry
Tuesday to Saturday 9:30 A.M. – 4:00 P.M.
A call ahead is recommended
(613) 283-8323

When visiting Greenburnie Antiques, cross the road to Rideau Antiques for an antiquing experience of an altogether different kind.

Recommended Reading:
Furniture Treasury, Wallace Nutting

47

Montague House

Weird, Wonderful and Whimsical

Bill Dobson lays the responsibility for his present taste in antiques squarely at the foot of *The Upper Canadian*, the trade journal for antique dealers and collectors.

Back in 1966 Bill was an impoverished schoolteacher, and out of necessity, he bought some used furniture. He knew nothing about antiques, but one of the pieces he bought was a round oak table. He

paid one dollar for it, and he sold it not long after for seventy-five dollars. This, he thought, was wonderful. Ten years later he quit teaching and went into the antique business full time, calling his shop Montague House after the township in which it is located.

Bill was collecting tools then, and he recalls that auctioneers used to sell a tool chest and its entire contents for just one bid. He has tinsmith's tools, blacksmith's tools, and woodworker's tools, and he entertains a whimsical dream about building an education centre on his property which would reconstruct the past.

In 1980 while Bill was still buying tools and selling early Canadiana, three other fellows in the antique business, Jan Bos, John Ford, and Tim Potter, established *The Upper Canadian*. Three years later Bill began to sell advertising for the newspaper. Then he bought a quarter share in the business. In 1988, full of enthusiasm about the future of the paper, he bought his three partners out. Today *The Upper Canadian* boasts a list of four thousand subscribers.

What is sometimes weird, says Bill, is the juggling act he has to perform. He still operates Montague House—specializing in early Canadian furniture, textiles, quality folk art, unusual accessories, and North

An Eastern Ontario corner cupboard is among Bill's choice of wonderful things.

The daily chores of our pioneering ancestors are quietly explained through the many tools they left behind: anvils, wool winders, butter churns....

American native items—but he also attends at least one hundred shows a year to promote the paper and keep up to date with the trade. He has taken *The Upper Canadian* from the east coast to the west and into the United States, and he has broadened its coverage to include all areas of collecting.

The paper has demanded that he be open-minded about all aspects of antiques and collecting. It has forced his tastes to become eclectic. As he learns more about subjects like the Arts and Crafts Movement, the Art Deco period, or pre-Confederation glass, he finds himself savouring it all. It's weird, it's wonderful, and it's whimsical, and he wouldn't want it any other way.

Montague House:
Bill Dobson
Three miles east of Smiths Falls through the Chambers Street subway
Open by chance or appointment
(613) 283-1168

For a subscription, write to *The Upper Canadian*, P.O. Box 653, Smiths Falls, Ontario, K7A 4T6.

Another Canadian antique publication is *Antique Showcase*, Peter and Barbara Sutton-Smith, P.O. Box 260, Bala, Ontario, P0C 1A0.

48

Tamarack Acres Antique Shoppe
A Feeling for Construction

It's the shape and the flow and the balance that mean everything to Gertie and Ronette when they look at a piece of Canadian country furniture.

Gertie Kennedy worked in time study before she moved to Black's Corners, just south of Ottawa, to a farm she named Tamarack Acres because of the preponderance of tamaracks on the property. She began to raise pigs, and was soon joined by Ronette Vines, a nurse before she became a pig farmer.

A grouping of antiques in the garden at Tamarack Acres.

When asked how they got into antiques, they answer together, "The winter of seventy-one." It was so severe that many a morning it took hours just to dig their way to the barn. They decided there had to be a better way to make a living on their beloved Tamarack Acres. The following summer they started doing upholstery and refinishing, some of it for Philip Shackleton, the author of *The Furniture of Old Ontario*, who taught them a great deal about Canadian antiques.

The construction of country furniture, though primitive, can be very appealing, says Gertie. It's difficult to explain the lure of elements of construction so simple yet so perfectly functional: shelves carefully joined with mortise-and-tenon joints, top and bottom boards painstakingly dovetailed to the sides of two-piece cupboards, numerous spool turnings with each spool hand-turned just slightly differently, bottom cutouts that have that extra flair—these are the details that delight you when you look at a country piece.

Take pegging, for example, a remarkable form of construction used in Quebec furniture. Armoires completely held together with wooden pegs will come apart when all the pegs are removed. "That's fine construction," says Gertie. And with Windsor chairs it's the splay of the legs, the rounding of the back slats, the angle at which the back spindles are attached to the slab seat, that all come together to give an overall pleasing look of balance and good workmanship. "Every old rocking chair is different," explains Gertie. "It's as if the maker measured the person, then built the perfect rocker to fit that person."

Gertie and Ronette believe in showing articles that are clean and safe and ready to place in your home and use. The furniture at Tamarack Acres has a durable finish. The accessories—glass, china, baskets, iron, tinware, treenware, toys and decoys—are all cleaned before appearing in the showroom.

Antiques are a long way from time study. When these things were constructed, says Gertie, it didn't matter how long it took; the job was done by a craftsman and it was done right.

Tamarack Acres Antique Shoppe:
G.A. Kennedy and R.E. Vines
Just west of Black's Corners on the 9th Line
Open Friday, Sunday and Monday 9:00 A.M. – 6:00 P.M., Saturday 9:00 A.M. – 5:00 P.M. Other days by appointment.
(613) 257-2078

A pine cupboard from Kaladar, Ontario (first quarter 19th century), is laden with an exceptional set of flow-blue china. In front is an arrowback rocker with perfect proportion and style.

49

Donohue and Bousquet
A Sterling Experience

Enter Donohue and Bousquet's in Ottawa and find yourself reflected on a hundred curved and belled and glowing surfaces. Silver has been the specialty of Arthur Bousquet and associate Collin O'Leary since 1985, although the business actually began in 1971, when Arthur and his wife, Lelia Donohue, bought the existing antique business of M. and Mme. Louis Leclerc in Quebec City. Ten years later they moved to Ottawa, a city Arthur describes as cosmopolitan, "an exciting place to buy and sell silver."

Silver is generally marked, and these markings are well documented. English silver has employed a hallmarking system since the thirteenth century. English, American and Canadian sterling is .925 silver with the remaining .075 a strengthening alloy, usually copper. Prior to 1865 the coin standard of .900 was used in America. European countries have varying sterling standards.

Design sells silver, whether sterling or Sheffield plate or silver plate, says Arthur. Of course, sterling is the most valuable. Sheffield commands a good price too, since it was the first method of plating. Discovered in 1740, Sheffield plating was done until 1840, when the electroplating process was developed.

Craftsmanship, condition, maker—all are to be considered when establishing the value of a piece of antique silver. Usefulness is also a consideration. Says Arthur, "A beer mug is more interesting to buyers than a baby cup." Other useful and therefore popular items are tea and coffee sets, candlesticks, trays, entrée dishes, and flatware. Arthur avoids buying engraved silver since engraving is a negative factor when he tries to sell the piece: no one wants silver with someone else's name on it.

Something not many people think about is the importance of the patina of antique silver. Old silver has an elegant glow that can only come with age. This patina can be spoiled with chemical cleaning, too much polishing, or replating. Arthur recommends that you hand-clean your silver very gently and—here's the good news—not too often.

Some firms are known for producing quality silver: Asprey and Garrard in England, Gorham of Rhode Island, Tiffany of New York, Reed and Barton of Massachusetts. In Canada, Birks is the name that has represented the best.

Arthur likes his stock to be earlier than 1900. He tries to research each piece and find out as much as he can about the item before selling it. This requires an extensive library of reference books explaining the markings of silver around the world. Arthur's careful, scholarly approach to his trade guarantees that your experience at Donohue and Bousquet's will be a sterling one.

Donohue and Bousquet:
Arthur Bousquet and Collin O'Leary
27 Hawthorne Avenue, Ottawa
Open Monday to Saturday 10:30 A.M. – 5:30 P.M.
(613) 232-5665

Recommended references for North American silver:
Canadian Silver, Silverplate and Related Glass, Doris and Peter Unitt
Guide to Marks on Early Canadian Silver 18th & 19th Century, John E Langton
The Encyclopedia of American Silver Manufacturers, Dorothy Rainwater

Gleaming, glistening, glowing silver.

The lustrous world of Donohue and Bousquet, antique silver specialists.

50

Architectural Antique Co.

Exquisite Stained Glass and the Tale of a Tub

Eric Cohen and Robert McNutt will go to any lengths to save an antique bathtub.

Eric opened the Architectural Antique Co. in 1968, and Robert began his own collection of architectural antiques when he was a teenager. These are bulky items, and you might well wonder how Robert stored them. "With great difficulty," he laughs. His bedroom had so many stained-glass windows, door frames, and fireplace mantels in it that he could just barely find his bed. For several years Robert and Eric found themselves racing each other to the next demolition site. Finally, in 1983, tired of being pursued, Eric invited Robert to join him in the business.

Stained-glass windows are one of the specialties of the Architectural Antique Co. Such windows were made from 1880 to 1930, explains Robert, but they enjoyed their greatest popularity in the first twenty-five years of that period. They were made with coloured and sculptered glass pieces soldered together with lead. The finest and most expensive windows were made in several thin glass layers rather than using one piece of glass for each section. This gave greater depth and brilliance to the colours. In North America such exquisite windows were made by the Tiffany or Lafarge companies.

Windows with hand-painted scenes, birds or portraits as focal points are very desirable today, and bevelled-glass windows are desirable but rare. Simply put, the more detailing in the window the better. Look for other features, such as heavy rippling in the glass and the incorporation of slag glass, dense and opalescent, in the design. Cut-glass jewels and iridescent rock-shaped glass add interest as well.

This architectural warehouse also has a large stock of fireplace mantels made anywhere from 1790 to 1920. Antique mantels were made in marble, granite and slate, as well as pine, basswood, poplar, ash, cherry, mahogany, and such exotic woods as lacewood. Mass-produced mantels are easy to recognize, explains Robert, since they were made in a standard five-foot-wide size. If you find a wider mantel you can be assured that it was custom-made. Mantels with mirrors incorporated above were made after 1890.

You will also find antique light fixtures in this shop, and Robert stresses that these are in their original finish. Doors and entrances, staircases and parts, unique antique hardware and even fine furniture are also part of the inventory.

The Architectural Antique Co. also stocks "exotic plumbing." Large, luxurious bathtubs, pull-chain toilets, and elegant marble shower stalls are all reminiscent of another time. Antique bathtubs can be six to seven feet long. Roman tubs were made with taps on the side, not the end, to facilitate long, luxurious soaks. Once Eric and Robert found a solid ceramic Roman bathtub in a house that was about to be

demolished. No matter how many men they employed, they found the tub was too heavy and awkward to lift. Refusing to give up, they hired a crane and hoisted it out of the house through an upstairs window.

When it comes to rescuing house fittings, the Architectural Antique Co. in Ottawa just won't be defeated.

ABOVE: Using architectural pieces from the past can create a distinctive decor.
FACING PAGE: Mouldings, mantels and rare lighting are preserved from the past to serve again in a new setting.

Architectural Antique Co.:
Eric Cohen and Robert McNutt
1240 Bank Street, Ottawa
Open weekdays 10:00 A.M. – 6:00 P.M., Saturdays
10:00 A.M. – 5:00 P.M., Sundays 11:00 – 5:00 P.M.
Best to phone ahead (613) 738-9243
Fax (613) 738 9782

Bank Street is *the* place for antiques in Ottawa.

Recommended reference:
The Victorian House Catalogue of 1900, reprinted by Sterling Publishing Co. Inc., New York, 1992.

For architectural antiques with a country flair try Balleycanoe and Co., John Sorensen, R.R. 4, Mallorytown, (613) 659-3874.